HOW TO EFFECTIVELY CO-PARENT WITH A NARCISSIST

A Practical Guide to Manage Conflict & Communication, Set Boundaries, Counteract Manipulation, Protect Your Children, and Support Your Mental Health

JENNA LEXINGTON

To my amazing boys,

Thank you for being my inspiration and my joy.

You're the reason I get up every day and keep pushing forward.

"I can be changed by what happens to me. But I refuse to be reduced by it."

Maya Angelou

A Special Gift for You

As a thank you for reading *How to Effectively Co-Parent with a Narcissist,* I have a special gift for you. It's a 36-page ebook titled *Navigating Emotional Triggers While Co-Parenting with a Narcissist,* and I'd love for you to have it—completely free.

This workbook is not just a collection of ideas but a practical guide packed with strategies that will empower you to stay calm and centered, no matter the challenges.

I appreciate your support, and I hope this workbook brings you even more clarity and peace in your co-parenting experience.

To get your free copy, head over to this site and join my mailing list:

Contents

Introduction

A few years ago, I sat alone in my room, feeling the weight of the walls around me. Usually, I'd be in a courtroom with my lawyer by my side, but because of COVID, I was logged into a Zoom call, waiting for the judge's decision. My lawyer's face was just a tiny square on the screen, voice muted.

Each minute dragged on. I would have felt supported in the courtroom with my lawyer next to me. But here, I felt disconnected and alone, like watching a movie about someone else's life. As I waited for the judge's decision, I felt isolated. I closed my eyes, took another deep breath, and focused back on the screen, ready to face whatever came next.

Outside, the world kept spinning as usual, but inside, everything felt like it was hanging by a thread. This was one of many challenging moments during my over three-year battle through a high-conflict divorce.

Little did I know that the challenges awaiting me during our post-divorce co-parenting journey would be just as stressful, if not more. Without my lawyer as a safety net, I was navigating the conflict alone. My ex's narcissistic tendencies made co-parenting a constant struggle. I wish I had something to prepare me for the storm that was about to unfold.

If you are also co-parenting with a narcissistic ex, I get what you're going through. The frustration from constant conflicts and loneliness because no one else understands—I've been there, too. Dealing with the back-and-forth arguments and the endless drama can be exhausting. You might feel like you're constantly walking on eggshells, trying to keep the peace while also trying to stand your ground. It's a tricky balance, and sometimes it feels like no matter what you do, it's never enough.

Having this book is like having a friend who's been through the same challenges of co-parenting with a narcissistic ex. It's filled with practical tips, heartfelt support, and real-life stories to help you manage conflicts, set boundaries, and care for yourself. By sharing experiences and giving you easy-to-follow advice, this book aims to help you create a stable, loving home for you and your kids while building resilience and finding a supportive community.

What makes this guide special is its mix of personal insights, collective wisdom from a community of people who have walked this path, and professional advice. This isn't just another self-help book; it's a toolkit for dealing with the unique challenges of co-parenting with a narcissist.

You'll dive into the ins and outs of narcissism, learn how to communicate in ways that keep your peace intact and find advice on protecting your rights. We'll provide practical tools like ready-to-use scripts for tricky conversations and tips for setting healthy boundaries.

As we move through this co-parenting journey, get ready to face emotional and practical challenges. This book will give you knowledge, strategies, and a sense of community. The road ahead may have its bumps, but it also offers chances for personal growth and peace.

Think of this as your first step toward a more peaceful and fulfilling life for you and your kids. Believe in your strength and resilience, and let this book guide you. Together, we can work toward a future where you feel empowered and at peace.

ONE

Understanding Narcissism

Okay, imagine you're about to go on a big adventure, like sailing a boat. Before you head out, you'd want to know if there will be a big storm or if the sea will be calm, right? Well, dealing with co-parenting when the other parent is a narcissist is kind of like that. You must understand what you're getting into to be ready for anything.

Now, narcissism isn't just a fancy word people use when someone loves to look at themselves in the mirror a lot. It's a real thing that affects how people act, especially in families. This chapter is here to help you understand what narcissism means. We'll discuss what makes someone a narcissist and how it shows up in real life, especially when it comes to parenting.

Think of it like this: if you know what to look for, it's easier to spot the signs. It's like having a treasure map when searching for hidden treasure. By understanding the traits and behaviors of a narcissist, you'll be able to see the challenges coming from a mile away. This means you can be ready to handle them and keep yourself and your kids safe and happy.

We'll break it down into simple, easy-to-understand pieces. We'll discuss what narcissism looks like and how it can affect parenting. And don't worry—we'll also share some tips on how to deal with it. By the end of this chapter, you'll feel more prepared and confident. You've got this, and we're here to help you every step of the way.

We'll figure out how to spot narcissistic behavior and what you can do to make things better for you and your kids. Remember, you're not alone in this; understanding is the first step to improving things.

1.1 Defining Narcissism

Alright, let's examine narcissism and its effects on our lives, especially co-parenting. Imagine a person who thinks they're the best at everything, needs constant praise, and doesn't care much about other people's feelings. That's a narcissist in a nutshell.

Narcissistic Personality Disorder, or NPD, is like having a super-sized ego without much empathy. People with NPD often think they're better than everyone else and crave constant admiration. They believe they're unique and special and can only be understood by or should hang out with other special or high-status people.

Narcissism can pop up in different ways. Here are some main traits and behaviors you might notice:

- Narcissists often act like they're the best at everything and deserve special treatment. They might brag about their achievements, even if they're not as impressive as they make them out to be. They feel entitled to the best of everything and believe others should cater to their needs without question.
- They need constant attention and compliments, always wanting to be the center of attention and getting upset if they don't receive enough praise. They heavily rely on others to boost their self-esteem, often boasting about their accomplishments or seeking people to flatter them.

- They struggle to understand or care about other people's feelings, often appearing indifferent or cruel in response to others' emotions or needs. They focus primarily on their own needs and desires, frequently exploiting or manipulating others without considering the impact on those individuals.

These traits can make any relationship challenging but incredibly difficult in a family dynamic. For instance, a narcissistic parent might push their child to be super successful, not for the child's benefit but to make themselves look good. They might brag about their child's achievements as if they were their own.

Narcissism can come in two flavors: overt and covert.

- **Overt** narcissists are what you might typically imagine a narcissist to be. They're loud, self-confident, and always seeking admiration. They openly show their entitlement and expect everyone to cater to them.
- **Covert** narcissists are more challenging to spot. They might seem shy or modest but secretly harbor grandiose fantasies. They often play the victim or use passive-aggressive behavior to manipulate others. This makes covert narcissism just as challenging in relationships, if not more so, because it's less prominent.

1.2 A Deeper Look at Covert Narcissism

Alright, let's dive a little deeper into covert narcissism because it's super important to understand just how tricky it can be. The thing with covert narcissists is that they're good at hiding in plain sight. Unlike the blatant, in-your-face narcissists, these folks keep their true nature under wraps. This makes them even harder to spot, which means that many people in relationships with them don't even realize what's happening. They might think something feels off but can't quite put their finger on it. That's why being with a covert narcissist can be so confusing—and, honestly, really dangerous.

To the outside world, a covert narcissist might look like the perfect partner. They can come across as caring, supportive, and attentive. They might be the kind of person who goes out of their way to help others, always with a smile, making everyone think they're just the most excellent person ever. But behind closed doors, it's a whole different story.

In private, a covert narcissist often tries to control and manipulate their partner in ways that are sneaky and hard to recognize. They don't need to yell or throw tantrums to get what they want. Instead, they rely on guilt, pity, or subtle mind games. These tactics might seem harmless initially, but they can be incredibly dangerous, especially if you don't realize what's happening.

One of the most frightening aspects of covert narcissism is that their true nature, including violent tendencies, often only comes out in private. While they maintain a calm, composed, and loving public persona, things can be very different behind closed doors. A covert narcissist might become verbally or even physically abusive when no one else is around. They know how to control their anger and hide their aggression from the outside world, making it hard for others to believe that such a "nice" person could be capable of such behavior.

Let's look at some examples that might help you spot a covert narcissist. Imagine your partner insists on managing all the finances. They might say, "I'm just better with numbers, and I don't want you to stress about it." On the surface, this seems caring, like they're trying to take a burden off your shoulders. But over time, you realize that you have no idea where your money is going, and any time you ask, they get defensive or dismissive. "Don't worry about it," they might say, "I'm taking care of us." This kind of control can leave you financially dependent and vulnerable, making it much harder to go if the relationship becomes more toxic.

Another example could be related to your social life. A covert narcissist might subtly isolate you from friends and family without you even realizing it. They might say, "I don't get along with your friends, but if you want to go out, I'll just stay home alone. It's fine."

This might make you feel guilty for wanting to spend time with others, so you start canceling plans to avoid making them feel bad. Over time, your world becomes smaller and smaller, revolving only around them. This isolation can be dangerous because it cuts you off from support systems, making it easier for the narcissist to maintain control.

Then there's the issue of health. A covert narcissist might downplay your concerns or dismiss your need for self-care. For example, if you mention feeling unwell or needing to see a doctor, they might say, "You're always worrying about nothing. You're fine. Just relax." On the surface, this might sound like they're trying to comfort you, but it's a way to minimize your needs and keep the focus on them. Over time, this could lead to serious health issues being ignored, all because your concerns are constantly belittled or dismissed.

Lastly, a covert narcissist might use your insecurities against you in a subtle yet damaging way. Suppose you're nervous about a big presentation at work. They might say, "I'm sure you'll do fine, but you know how you get when you're nervous. Just don't mess up this time." This might seem like they're trying to motivate you, but it's planting seeds of doubt, making you feel even more insecure. When you don't perform as well as you'd hoped, they might offer false sympathy, saying, "I knew you'd struggle with this, but it's okay. I still love you." This manipulation can erode your self-confidence, making you more reliant on their approval and less confident in your abilities.

Another common tactic is playing the victim. Covert narcissists love to make you feel sorry for them. They might talk about how they've been mistreated in the past or how no one understands them, making you feel like you need to take care of them or put their needs above your own. This keeps you off balance because you're always trying to make them feel better while they're quietly pulling the strings.

Because covert narcissism is so hard to identify, it can do a lot of damage before you even realize what's going on. The emotional manipulation can make you feel like you're walking on eggshells all the time. You might start doubting your feelings, thinking that maybe you're the one who's too sensitive or demanding. This constant self-doubt can take a toll on your mental and emotional health.

And since covert narcissists are so good at keeping up appearances, it can be challenging to get support from others. Friends and family might not understand what you're going through because your partner seems kind and loving. This can leave you feeling isolated and even more confused.

If you're reading this and thinking, "This sounds familiar," it's essential to take a step back and look at your relationship. Ask yourself if you're always the one who has to apologize, make sacrifices, or boost your partner's ego. Do you feel like you're constantly trying to please them, but it's never enough? Do they act differently in public than they do at home? If the answer is yes, you might be dealing with a covert narcissist.

The first step is recognizing what's happening. Once you do, it's essential to set boundaries and protect yourself. Don't hesitate to contact trusted friends, family, or a therapist for support. Remember, you deserve to be in a relationship where you feel valued, respected, and free to be yourself—without constantly walking on eggshells.

1.3 Why Being with a Covert Narcissist Can Be Worse

Being with a covert narcissist can be more harmful than being with an overt one. Here's why:

1. **Mind Games:** Covert narcissists are pros at making you question what's real. They might make you feel like you're the one with the problem, not them. Over time, this can mess with your head and make it hard to trust your feelings.
2. **Constant Criticism:** They might always find little ways to put you down, making you less confident. They often

make you feel you're to blame for everything, affecting your self-esteem.

3. **Isolation:** They might try to cut you off from your friends and family by making you think they're the only ones who care about you. This makes it easier for them to control you.

4. **Emotional Coldness:** Instead of getting angry, covert narcissists might ignore you as a way to punish you. This can be painful because it makes you feel alone and desperate to regain their approval.

5. **Unrealistic Demands:** They often expect too much from you, making you feel like you're constantly failing. This can make you feel hopeless and unhappy.

If you're co-parenting with a covert narcissist, things get even more challenging. They might try to make themselves look like the better parent, subtly undermining you and making the kids feel sorry for them. This can create an unhealthy situation where the kids are caught in the middle and being used to feed the narcissist's need for attention.

Real-Life Examples

Let's examine some examples to understand how these traits play out in real life.

Sarah's Story Sarah is a mom co-parenting with an overtly narcissistic ex-partner. Her ex constantly needs admiration and believes he's always right. He makes decisions about their kids without consulting Sarah and ignores her opinions. This strains their co-parenting and stresses the kids, who feel caught between their parents.

John's Story John, on the other hand, has a covertly narcissistic ex-partner. She often plays the victim and manipulates situations to gain sympathy. She subtly turns their children against John, suggesting he's uncaring or unavailable. This manipulation isn't apparent but profoundly impacts how the kids see their dad.

Understanding these traits and behaviors is crucial. It helps you recognize patterns, anticipate issues, and devise strategies that prioritize your and your children's well-being. As you continue through this co-parenting journey, keep these insights in mind. They're the first step in moving from merely surviving to truly thriving.

1.4 How Narcissism Affects Your Relationships

Imagine living in a house where the walls keep shifting, and the rooms change places every time you turn around. That's what being in a relationship with a narcissist can feel like. It's confusing and stressful and makes you doubt everything, including yourself. One minute, everything seems fine, and the next, you're caught in a storm of accusations and mind games.

The chaos doesn't just affect you; it also hits the kids hard. Living with a narcissistic parent is like trying to predict the weather during a hurricane. Sometimes, the parent is super controlling, dictating every little thing. Other times, they're neglectful, acting like the kids don't exist. This hot-and-cold behavior can make kids feel anxious, withdrawn, angry, and aggressive.

Children with a narcissistic parent might:

- **Withdraw**: They might pull back from social interactions, becoming quiet and withdrawn, trying to stay out of the way.
- **Act Out**: They might lash out, showing aggression because they're confused and hurt.
- **Seek Attention**: They might do anything for the narcissistic parent's approval, even if it means changing who they are to fit what the parent wants.

Kids learn to adapt to survive, but these adaptations can lead to emotional issues later in life. They're trying to navigate a maze of mixed signals and shifting expectations, which can be incredibly destabilizing. We will discuss this further in chapter 5.

Dealing with a narcissist can feel like being on a roller coaster, especially when you're co-parenting from separate households. You're constantly bracing for the next twist or drop, and it's exhausting. The ups and downs don't just affect you; they ripple through the entire family, especially the kids. While you can't control what goes on at their place, you can create a stable and loving environment at home. Start by establishing predictable routines. Having a daily schedule provides a sense of security for your kids, which is especially important if things are chaotic with their other parent. Knowing what to expect each day can be incredibly comforting for them.

Encourage your kids to talk about their feelings and really listen to them. Let them know it's okay to feel sad, angry, or confused and that you're there to support them. Open and honest conversations can help them process their experiences and feel understood.

Don't hesitate to seek outside support. Family counselors and parenting experts can offer valuable advice and strategies to help you and your children navigate this difficult situation. Professional guidance can provide tools to cope with the challenges and build resilience.

While you can't change the narcissist's behavior, you can create a protective buffer in your home. This means setting boundaries and focusing on what you can control—your actions and reactions. By doing this, you're helping to maintain your family's emotional and psychological health.

1.5 Narcissists on Co-parenting

One of the biggest headaches is the constant fighting. Even the most minor decisions can blow up into huge arguments. Imagine just trying to decide on weekend plans for your child. What should be a simple discussion turns into a battle. The narcissist sees any disagreement as a threat to their control and reacts by escalating the conflict. This isn't just about winning but their need for attention and validation. These arguments build up, creating a stressful environment where everyone feels on edge. The kids, stuck in the middle, often feel anxious and stressed. They might start acting out at school or having trouble sleeping because of all the tension at home.

Narcissists love having control. They might try to manage everything about the kids' lives—from what they wear to who they spend time with. This can show up as them constantly criticizing your parenting or ignoring your input, even in front of the kids. For example, they might sign the kids up for activities that fall on your parenting time without discussing it first. Or they might make big decisions about holidays without even talking to you, disregarding what you think or what the kids want.

Manipulation comes in many forms when dealing with a narcissist. One sneaky trick they use is called triangulation. This is where they try to make the kids take sides, often turning them against you. They might say things like, "Your mom never lets you do fun stuff," or "Your dad doesn't care about what you want." This can leave the kids feeling anxious and confused, not knowing who to trust, which can mess up their relationship with both parents.

Another common tactic is gatekeeping, where the narcissist controls when and how you see your kids. They might suddenly change plans or make it difficult for you to spend time with the kids, using them as pawns to manipulate and control you. For example, they might agree to a weekend visit and then, at the last minute, claim the kids are sick or have a "surprise" family event, making you miss out on your time together. It's a way for them to keep you in check and ensure they hold all the power, which can be incredibly frustrating and heartbreaking.

Another significant issue is the narcissist's inconsistent parenting. One day, they might be super strict, enforcing rules to show they're in charge. They're overly lenient or indifferent the next day based on their mood or needs. This kind of flip-flopping confuses the kids. They never know what to expect, which makes it hard for them to feel safe and secure. Imagine a child who receives harsh punishment for a small mistake one day, but the same behavior goes ignored the next day. This inconsistency can complicate their understanding of boundaries and rules crucial for healthy emotional development.

Narcissists often use the legal system as a weapon. They might drag you into endless legal battles over custody or make unfounded accusations to make you look bad. These fights are not just about winning custody; they're about maintaining control and keeping you on your toes. This legal harassment is draining—emotionally, mentally, and financially. It can go on for years, making it hard for you to move forward and focus on what matters: your kids' well-being.

Money is another tool narcissists use to manipulate and control. They might try to make you financially dependent on them by controlling the purse strings tightly. For example, they could withhold child support payments to punish you or dictate how you should spend every dollar. They could deny paying their share of extra-curricular expenses, claiming they never agreed to the activities. This financial abuse extends their control over you and the children, even after separation. We will discuss how to handle this financial abuse in a later chapter.

Narcissists also love to undermine your authority as a parent. They might criticize your decisions in front of the kids or twist situations to make you look like the "bad guy." For example, you might say no to a last-minute sleepover because it's a school night, and they'll say, "I would have let you go, but your mom/dad always says no to fun things." This kind of behavior can mess with the kids' heads. They start feeling confused and stressed, caught in a battle they didn't sign up for. It's unfair and burdens them a heavy emotional burden, making it challenging to trust either parent and have a healthy relationship.

Narcissists often pull out all the stops to win the kids' loyalty, showering them with excessive gifts or making grand promises they never intend to keep. They're trying to buy the kids' affection, trying to come across as the "fun" parent. They might promise an expensive gadget or an extravagant birthday party, but when the time comes, there's always an excuse— "I couldn't find it," or "The timing wasn't right." It's a manipulation tactic that leaves the kids feeling disappointed and confused.

Conversely, they might badmouth you and undermine your relationship with the kids. They might comment, "Your mom/dad never lets you do anything fun," or "I don't think they care about your interests." These remarks can mess with a child's mind, making them question who to trust and where they stand with each parent. It creates an unnecessary emotional tug-of-war, confusing your kids and making it hard for you to reassure them when they constantly hear mixed messages.

Finding the right therapist for your child is vital in situations like this. A therapist who understands the nuances of these dynamics can make a big difference. You want someone who not only has experience with kids but also has specialized training in trauma and domestic violence. They must understand the specific challenges your child is facing, not just attribute everything to typical parental disagreements. This expertise helps the therapist provide the proper support, helping your child work through their feelings, develop healthy coping skills, and build resilience. It's about ensuring your child has a safe space to navigate these complex emotions and become more assertive on the other side.

Unfortunately, some therapists without proper training might misinterpret the signs and patterns of abuse as just lousy parenting days, missing the bigger picture. This can lead to your child not getting the support they need. So, finding a therapist with the right expertise ensures your child is understood and cared for in the best way possible. It's all about giving your kiddo the understanding and help they deserve.

1.6 Anticipating Challenges

Narcissists have triggers—things that make them react negatively. These triggers often include anything that threatens their self-image or sense of control. For example, correcting them in front of others or setting firm boundaries can lead to explosive outbursts. It's not just about what you say or do but how it makes them feel. They don't like feeling less in control or admired. Knowing these triggers helps you plan to avoid unnecessary fights and manage the ones you can't prevent more effectively.

One helpful tool is scenario planning. This means thinking ahead about situations that might come up and how you can handle them. Imagine you're about to do a custody exchange or go to a school event. If your ex-partner hates public corrections, discuss any issues privately. Or, if you think they might make a scene in front of others, bring along a neutral third party or communicate through notes or messages instead of face-to-face. This way, you can keep things calmer and more controlled.

One of the most challenging but essential things you can do is stay calm when your ex tries to provoke you. Narcissists can be unpredictable and may say or do things to get a reaction. If you remain calm and collected, you prevent the situation from escalating. Try techniques like deep breathing, pausing before you respond, and sticking to the facts instead of getting emotional. Remember, the goal isn't to win an argument but to keep the peace for the sake of your kids.

Another critical strategy is to keep detailed records. Document everything—conversations, decisions, interactions. This can be crucial if your ex tries to manipulate situations or make false accusations. For example, keep a log of who takes the kids to their activities or doctor appointments. This evidence can protect you from legal disputes and show you're a responsible parent.

Sometimes, you'll need extra help. Don't hesitate to get legal advice, especially when dealing with custody issues, financial disputes, or boundary violations. A lawyer can help you enforce your rights and protect your family. For example, if your ex keeps breaking the rules you've agreed on, having a lawyer send a formal warning can be more effective than handling it alone.

Therapy is also a great resource. Both you and your kids might benefit from talking to a professional. Therapy provides a safe space to express feelings and learn coping strategies. It helps you deal with the emotional stress of co-parenting with a narcissist, ensuring that you can stay strong and supportive of your children.

By anticipating and planning for challenges, you create a more stable environment for yourself and your children. This proactive approach helps you focus on what matters—raising healthy, happy kids, even amid complicated family dynamics. It's not about eliminating all the storms but learning to sail through them confidently and carefully.

1.7 Breaking Myths

Alright, let's dive into some myths about narcissists, especially when it comes to parenting. These myths can mess with how we understand and handle these tricky relationships. Let's break them down to protect and support our kids better.

Myth #1: Narcissists Are Always Obvious Bullies

Many people think that narcissists are always in-your-face bullies, showing their true colors in loud and clear ways. Sure, some narcissists are like that, but many are much sneakier. Their abuse can be super subtle, like a whispered insult that sticks with you or a disappointed look that makes you feel worthless. For example, a narcissistic parent might not scream at their child for a bad grade but might sigh and say, "I expected more from you." This kind of behavior doesn't leave physical scars but can deeply hurt a child's self-esteem.

Myth #2: Young Kids Are Not Aware of Parental Narcissism

Some people believe that little kids are too young to notice or be affected by their parents' narcissistic behavior. Even very young kids are like little emotional sponges. They soak up their parents' moods and actions. When a parent is emotionally unavailable or constantly changing moods, it can affect a child's development. These kids might become anxious, act out, or even start copying the narcissistic behaviors they see, thinking that's how people act. Early childhood is essential for learning healthy relationships so that these negative influences can have long-lasting effects.

Myth #3: Narcissists Can't Love Their Kids

Another big myth is that narcissists don't love their children. They can love, but their love is often conditional and self-centered. They might shower their child with attention when it makes them look good, like bragging about the child's soccer goals to other parents. But if the child isn't excelling in a way that boosts the narcissist's ego, the affection might disappear. This kind of love confuses kids because it teaches them that they must earn love through achievements rather than being loved just for who they are.

TWO

Legal Rights and Strategies

Navigating the legal maze of divorce and custody can feel overwhelming, especially with a narcissistic ex. In this chapter, we'll break down the essentials of your legal rights and the strategies you need to protect yourself and your children. If you're still contemplating or are in the middle of a lengthy divorce process, you'll want to pay special attention here. From understanding your rights in property and financial matters to preparing for custody battles, we'll guide you through the key aspects you need to know. We'll also cover practical tips for gathering evidence and handling financial disputes. This chapter is about empowering you with the knowledge and tools to confidently face the legal challenges ahead and build a secure future for your family.

2.1 Understanding Your Rights

Understanding your rights helps you navigate the divorce process more efficiently and ensures you receive fair treatment. Pay attention to the discussion on property, child custody, and financial support. Each has specific laws to protect everyone's interests and ensure fairness.

Property Rights

Splitting up what you've accumulated during your marriage is usually about equitable distribution. This means the court aims to divide things fairly, not necessarily equally. They consider factors like each person's financial situation, contributions, and future needs.

With a narcissistic ex, property division can feel more like a power struggle than a legal process. They might try to manipulate the situation to make it seem like they contributed more or hide assets to reduce your share. Sometimes, they'll drag out the process to create unnecessary conflict and stress you out. That's why knowing your rights and being prepared is so important.

Start by gathering all your financial documents—bank statements, tax returns, property deeds, and records of big purchases. Having everything organized helps you show what you've contributed and where you stand financially. Also, make sure you understand the difference between marital and nonmarital property. Marital property includes anything acquired during the marriage, while nonmarital property covers stuff you owned before getting married or received as a gift or inheritance. Sometimes, these lines can get blurred, like if you used an inheritance to buy a family home. Knowing what counts as marital property can help you make a strong case for what you're entitled to.

Negotiation and mediation can be helpful but tricky when dealing with a narcissist. They might use mediation to twist things in their favor. That's why having a strong lawyer is invaluable. They can navigate these tricky waters, offer solid advice, and stand up for your interests.

Keep focused on the facts and let your lawyer handle the back-and-forth. This helps you avoid getting sucked into emotional traps that could derail the process. The goal is to get a fair division of property that reflects what you've contributed and what you'll need moving forward. You can protect yourself from manipulative tactics by being thorough with your documentation, understanding what counts as marital property, getting professional help, and keeping your emotions in check. This preparation helps during the property division process and sets the tone for future interactions, helping you focus on creating a stable and secure future for yourself and your kids.

Financial Support

Financial support is a critical piece of the puzzle when navigating the tricky waters of a high-conflict divorce. This includes alimony and child support, which aren't about punishment but about recognizing that both face post-divorce financial realities. The goal is to ensure you and your children have the financial resources to maintain stability and well-being.

Being well-prepared and proactive is crucial to protecting yourself and your children. Start by gathering all necessary financial documents. Detailed documentation is your best friend here; it helps paint a clear picture of the financial situation, making it harder for the narcissist to manipulate the facts.

Working with a forensic accountant can be incredibly beneficial. These professionals specialize in uncovering hidden assets and income, which is often necessary when dealing with a narcissists who might not be forthcoming about their finances. They can provide a comprehensive view of your ex's financial situation, ensuring that support calculations are fair and accurate.

Understanding your financial needs and those of your children is also vital. Create a detailed budget including all expenses, from everyday living to education and medical expenses. This budget will be an essential tool in court to calculate the financial support you'll provide or receive.

Having a skilled family law attorney on your side is crucial. An attorney experienced in high-conflict divorces can navigate the complexities of financial support, ensuring that your needs are communicated and well-represented. They can also help enforce support orders if your ex tries to avoid payments.

Legal tools like wage garnishment can be effective in ensuring regular support payments. If your ex is employed, the court can order their employer to withhold child support or alimony directly from their paycheck, ensuring you receive the support you're entitled to without constantly chasing after payments.

After the divorce, be prepared for the narcissist to find creative ways to avoid their financial responsibilities. They might interpret the court order favorably, looking for loopholes or ambiguous wording to justify not paying you. Expect them to argue about what constitutes income, try to hide new sources of revenue, or claim they can't afford payments due to sudden, suspicious financial hardships.

Stay vigilant and document everything. Keep meticulous records of non-payment or late payments and any communications regarding financial support. If necessary, be ready to return to court to enforce the support order. Your attorney can help you with contempt motions or modifications to ensure the order is clear and enforceable.

Custody Arrangements

Let's discuss custody arrangements because they're a big part of co-parenting. Custody isn't just about where your kids will live; it also involves who makes the critical decisions about their lives, like their education, healthcare, and other major life choices. When your ex has a narcissistic streak, navigating these waters can be super challenging. They might use custody discussions as a way to control or manipulate you rather than focusing on what's best for the kids.

You must stay sharp and aware that your ex might not prioritize the children's well-being. Instead, they might use various tactics to maintain power over you. This could include making false accusations, dragging out court proceedings unnecessarily, or even trying to turn the kids against you. It's a lot to handle, but being well-prepared can make a huge difference.

Start by knowing your legal rights and preparing thoroughly. Keep detailed records of everything—every conversation, every incident where your ex tries to manipulate or control the situation, and any evidence that shows your active role and commitment as a parent. This meticulous documentation can be a game-changer in court, helping to demonstrate your suitability as a custodial parent and counter any false claims your ex might make.

Understanding the difference between physical and legal custody is vital. Physical custody decides where the children live, while legal custody involves significant decisions about their upbringing. Sometimes, a narcissistic ex might fight for legal custody just to keep control and disrupt your life, even if they're not genuinely interested in making those decisions. That's why having a clear and detailed parenting plan is essential. This plan should cover everything, from visitation schedules to who makes what decisions. The more specific you are, the less room there is for manipulation. For example, spell out the exact times for exchanges, how you will handle holidays and vacations, and even how to resolve any disputes.

Work with your lawyer. They can guide you through the legal maze, help you build a strong case, and develop a strategy that keeps your children's stability and well-being front and center. Remember the emotional side, too. Involving a child psychologist or counselor can be invaluable. These professionals can provide insights into your children's needs, offer support during the transition, and even serve as impartial witnesses to your ex's behavior in court.

Most importantly, keep open and honest communication with your kids. Encourage them to share their feelings and let them know you're there for them no matter what. A safe and stable environment with you can make a difference in their emotional health.

State-Specific Laws

Understanding state-specific laws is imperative because divorce and custody rules can vary greatly depending on where you live. These laws impact everything from the divorce filing process to the details of custody arrangements and financial support. For example, some states require couples to live separately for a certain period before they can officially file for divorce, while others don't have this requirement. In some places, the courts lean toward joint custody, meaning both parents share responsibility. In contrast, the courts might focus more on the primary caregiver's role when deciding custody in other states.

It's imperative to know what the laws are in your state because they can shape how you approach your situation. This might involve researching independently, consulting with a local lawyer who knows the ins and outs of your state's legal system, or contacting state legal aid organizations for help. By understanding the specific laws where you live, you can better navigate the legal process and make informed decisions about your next steps.

Finding the Right Lawyer

Let's explore finding the right lawyer. This is a big deal, especially when you're dealing with a narcissistic ex. You need a lawyer who understands high-conflict divorces because they can make a difference. They're not just there for legal advice; they can also give you tips on handling negotiations and court appearances, which can be super intimidating.

Now, high-conflict divorces take time. They can drag on for years, so you must consider how to afford legal help for the long haul. Those super expensive lawyers who charge by the hour for every phone call and email? Yeah, they can drain your wallet fast. You might run out of funds and have to represent yourself (pro se). You want to avoid this. Instead, look for a lawyer who offers a flat fee or a payment plan. This way, you know what you're paying and won't get hit with surprise bills.

If money is tight, don't worry. Many states have legal aid services or organizations offering reduced-cost legal help for qualified people. These places ensure you get the support you need without breaking the bank.

When looking for a lawyer, asking the right questions is essential. Find out if they have experience with high-conflict divorces and narcissistic exes. Ask how they handle cases and their strategy for your situation. It's also good to see if they have experience with high-conflict custody cases because that can be another battle.

Also, think about the personality fit. You'll spend a lot of time with this person, so you need to feel comfortable with them. They should be someone who listens to you, understands your concerns, and makes you feel supported. If you don't feel that connection, it's okay to keep looking.

Remember, your lawyer is part of your support team, but they're not the only members. Surround yourself with friends, family, and maybe even a therapist who can help you through this tough time. A solid support system can make a huge difference in handling stress and emotional ups and downs.

A good lawyer will help you see the big picture. They'll help you stay focused on what's best for you and your kids in the long run, not just on winning every little battle. Sometimes, that means making tough choices and compromises, but with the right lawyer, you can confidently navigate these decisions.

Finding the correct legal representation is like finding the right tool for the job. It makes everything more accessible and more manageable. Take your time, ask questions, and find someone who will fight for you and your kids every step of the way.

2.2 Custody Battles

Mental Preparation

Imagine you're at the start of a big, challenging hike, looking up at a steep trail ahead. That's what a custody battle with a narcissist can feel like—a long and arduous journey that requires a lot of preparation. Your ex might pull stunts, like twisting the truth or acting like the victim to get what they want. It can feel like you're in a game where the rules keep changing. But don't worry—if you prepare well, you can stay grounded and deal with whatever comes your way.

First, let's talk about getting your head in the right place. Think of it as putting on your best hiking gear. You need to stay strong and realistic. Stress management techniques like mindfulness, meditation, or even yoga can help you keep cool. It's important to understand that this legal process might take some time, and things might not always go as planned. Knowing this can help you stay calm when things get tricky. Be ready for your ex to lie or twist facts to make themselves look good. Knowing these tactics, you can focus on the truth and what's best for your kids.

Gathering Evidence

Let's start with gathering evidence. This step is about showing the court that you're the best parent for your kids. It's about proving your side and clearly showing the stable and loving home you provide. This could include documenting daily activities, collecting statements from people who know your family, and anything else that shows your involvement in your kids' lives. It might seem overwhelming, but ensuring the court sees how committed you are to your children's well-being is essential.

First, let's talk about character references. These are like your cheerleaders. They see how awesome you are with your kids every day. Maybe your child's teacher has noticed that you always attend parent-teacher conferences. Or perhaps your kid's doctor has seen how you handle those stressful visits with calm and care. Close friends and family who've seen you in action are also great. They can all write letters or even speak in court about what a loving, dedicated parent you are. These references are super important because they show the court you're not just talking the talk – you're walking the walk.

Next up is documentation. It might sound tedious, but this part is crucial. Think of it like keeping a journal, specifically for all your interactions with your ex. Grab a notebook or start a new document on your computer and note everything down. Record the dates, times, and details of every conversation. Was there an argument about your child's school? Write it down. Did your ex refuse a recommended medical evaluation or medication? Make a note of that, too. The more details you include, the better. This isn't just about remembering things – it's about creating a comprehensive record that can help show the court what's going on. In the next section, we'll discuss organizing all the documentation you collect.

Another thing to remember is to save all your communication. This means texts, emails, and even voicemails. If your ex sends a nasty message or makes unreasonable demands, don't delete it. Save it and add it to your records. Screenshots can be a lifesaver here. Just make sure you back everything up in case your phone or computer decides to have a bad day.

Photos and videos can also be part of your evidence toolkit. Did you take your kids to the park and have a great day out? Snap a few photos. Did your child make a fantastic drawing at home? Take a picture. These small moments show the positive, loving environment you provide for your kids.

Documentation is your best friend in a custody battle. Later in this chapter, we'll discuss what to document, how to do it, and when to keep those records handy. Now, this can all feel overwhelming. But remember, you're not alone. Lean on your support network— friends, family, and even support groups. They can offer advice and encouragement and sometimes even help you keep track of things.

Gathering evidence is like putting together a puzzle. Each piece, whether a character reference, a documented interaction, or a saved text message, helps build the bigger picture of who you are as a parent. This picture will help you stand firm in court.

So, take a deep breath, gather your tools, and know you're doing everything possible to protect and provide for your children. You've got this!

Custody Evaluations

This part of the journey can be intense, so being prepared is good. Professionals conduct custody evaluations by examining your family situation to decide what's best for your kids. It's like having someone watch you closely and then report back on what they see. Sounds nerve-wracking, right? But don't worry—we'll go through this step by step.

First, let's get one thing straight: custody evaluations are expensive. We're talking about a lot of money. So, if there's a way to avoid it, try that first. But sometimes, you just can't avoid it. If you find yourself in that position, remember this: custody evaluators are not your friends. They are there to observe and report, not to take sides. So, it's crucial to stay calm and focused.

When you're going through an evaluation, consistency is your best friend. Show that you're a stable, caring parent. That means sticking to your routines, keeping your home environment positive, and showing genuine love and care for your kids. Evaluators look for signs that you can provide a steady, nurturing home.

Now, here's a big tip – do not badmouth your ex. It might be tempting, especially if your ex has done awful things, but evaluators are looking for facts, not personal attacks. If you start ranting about your ex, it can make you look bad, too. Stick to the facts. If there are issues you need to raise, talk about specific behaviors and how they impact your kids. For example, instead of saying, "My ex is manipulative," you could say, "There have been instances where my ex has pressured the kids to take sides, which has caused them a lot of stress."

Having evidence of your ex's problematic behavior is crucial. This is where all that documentation you've been gathering comes in handy. Text messages, emails, notes from teachers or doctors – anything that shows a pattern of behavior can be constructive. If there have been instances of abuse, ensure you have all that documented and ready to present. But again, stick to the facts. Describe what happened, when, and how it affected the children.

During the evaluation, be open and honest. Answer questions directly and provide as much detail as you can. If you try to hide things or stretch the truth, it could bite you. Trained evaluators spot inconsistencies, so honesty is the best policy.

Remember, the goal of the evaluation is to figure out what's best for your kids. Keep that in mind throughout the process. Focus on their well-being above all else. This means being flexible and willing to work with the other parent, even if it's tough.

Custody evaluations can feel like a spotlight shining directly on you and your family. It's stressful, no doubt about it. But if you stay calm, stick to the facts, and show that you are a loving, responsible parent, you can confidently navigate this part of the journey.

Guardian Ad Litem (GAL)

Due to the high-conflict nature of divorcing a narcissist, the court will most likely require a Guardian Ad Litem or GAL. GALs are your child's legal representatives during a custody battle. Narcissistic exes tend to turn every little thing into a struggle, making it hard to reach agreements. This makes it even more crucial to have a GAL who can cut through the chaos and focus on what truly matters: your children's well-being. They hear your kids' voices in court and look out for their best interests. Here's what you need to know.

First, understand that the GAL is not on your or your ex's side. They focus solely on what's best for the kids. They'll gather information from everyone involved – you, your ex, your kids, teachers, doctors, and anyone else who might provide insight into your family situation. They're putting together a puzzle to see the whole picture.

It's essential to ask for GAL recommendations from local support groups. Lawyers who serve as GALs focus their training on the law, and many lack training in domestic violence. Personal recommendations from others who have been in similar situations can be invaluable. They can point you toward GALs who are experienced and empathetic and, just as importantly, steer you away from those who might not be as helpful.

Make sure you stay on the good side of the GAL. They hold a lot of power and serve as the judge's eyes and ears throughout the divorce process. Knowing who to avoid can save you a lot of stress and ensure you get the best support for your kids.

When the GAL visits your home, it's crucial to be yourself and show that you're a stable and loving parent. Keep your home environment clean and welcoming. Ensure your kids follow their routines and show how much you care for them. The GAL will notice how you interact with your kids, how comfortable they are around you, and how well you meet their needs.

Just like with custody evaluations, avoid badmouthing your ex to the GAL. Stick to the facts. If there are concerns, explain them calmly and provide any documentation you have. For example, if your ex has missed a lot of visits, show the GAL your records. If there have been incidents of concern, have your evidence ready. The GAL is looking for concrete information, not personal attacks.

The GAL will also talk to your kids. Prepare them for this in a gentle, honest way. Let them know that the GAL wants to ensure they're okay and happy. Encourage your kids to speak openly, but don't coach them on what to say. The GAL wants to hear their genuine thoughts and feelings.

Remember, the GAL's report can significantly impact the court's decisions. The court takes their recommendations very seriously, so approach this part of the process with care and honesty. The GAL will report to the court about what they think is best for your kids based on the information they have gathered.

The Court's Perspective

The judge's main job is to ensure your children are healthy, safe, and happy. So, it's super important that you show how you can provide a loving and stable home for them.

First off, remember never to call your ex a narcissist in court. Judges don't like it when people throw medical terms around without a professional's opinion. Instead, focus on their behavior and how it affects your kids. For instance, if your ex frequently cancels plans at the last minute or speaks negatively about you in front of the kids, these actions can cause confusion and emotional distress for your children.

Now, let's dive into what the judge is looking for. They want to see that you're the rock for your kids, someone who can offer them a steady, loving environment. Talk about the routines you've set up at home. Do you have a consistent bedtime? Do you sit down for meals together? These little details paint a picture of a nurturing home where your kids can feel safe and loved.

But what about your ex's behavior? If your ex's actions are harmful, you need to show that, but without using labels like "narcissist." Stick to the facts. For instance, if your ex frequently yells at you during exchanges, provide examples of how that creates a tense and stressful environment for your children. Or, if your ex frequently yells at them for minor mistakes, provide examples of how that creates anxiety or low self-esteem in your children.

Judges also care a lot about your child's emotional well-being. They want to know you're attuned to your kids' feelings and needs. Talk about how you encourage your kids to express their emotions and how you support them when they're feeling down. Maybe you've set up regular check-ins with your kids, where they can talk about anything bothering them. Or perhaps you've sought out counseling to help them navigate their feelings.

Another biggie is safety. If there have been any incidents where your ex's behavior has put your kids at risk, document them and present them. Again, stick to the facts and avoid inflammatory language. If there's been verbal abuse, keep records of any messages or emails. If there's been neglect, note the times and circumstances. Your goal is to show the judge that your home is a haven where your kids are safe and secure.

One last thing to remember is that judges like to see cooperation. Even if your ex makes things difficult, showing that you're willing to co-parent effectively can go a long way. It's about putting your kids first, always.

Legal Protections

Let's talk about getting extra help from the law when things get tough. Sometimes, dealing with a narcissistic ex can go beyond the usual headaches and turn into something more serious, like abuse or nasty manipulation. In these cases, you might need some legal shields, like restraining orders or supervised visitation. This isn't just legal mumbo jumbo; it's about keeping you and your kids safe.

So, how do you go about this? First, if there's any proof that your ex has made threats or has been emotionally abusive, you'll want to gather it up. This could be nasty text messages, emails, or even notes from times they've yelled or said hurtful things in front of the kids. Having this kind of evidence can be super helpful.

With this proof, you can go to court and ask for a restraining order. This is a legal way to keep your ex away from you and the kids, at least temporarily. It can provide some breathing room and peace of mind.

Another option is supervised visitation. This means that someone else monitors the kids when your ex visits them. It can ensure that the visits are safe and don't create more drama or manipulation opportunities.

Getting these protections can be challenging and stressful. But remember, it's all about creating a safe and stable environment for your kids and yourself. You don't have to do it alone, either. Reach out to local support groups or legal aid services for guidance. They can help you understand the steps and give you the support you need to get through them.

Ultimately, having these legal protections in place can make a big difference. It's like having an extra layer of armor to shield you and your kids from the negative impacts of dealing with a narcissistic ex. And with that protection, you can focus more on building a healthier, happier life for your family.

2.3 Documentation and Evidence

Imagine you're gearing up for a big game. You wouldn't go in without a game plan and the right gear, right? Well, when you're in a legal battle, especially with a narcissist, your game plan is your documentation. Think of it as your house's foundation; nothing stands firm without it.

Let's start with the basics. Documenting isn't just jotting down random notes. It's about creating a clear, detailed, and chronological record of every interaction with your narcissistic ex. This means writing down every conversation, whether it's in person, over the phone, via text, or email. Date and time each entry, and explain what you discussed and the decisions you made. This level of detail is crucial. It paints a clear picture of what's happening and can be helpful during custody evaluations or court hearings where it's your word against theirs.

But don't stop at just texts and emails. Any kind of communication can be evidence. Social media posts, comments, or messages can show patterns of emotional abuse, harassment, or manipulation. For example, save screenshots of these communications if your ex frequently sends abusive texts or messages on social media. Third-party testimonies are also powerful. If friends or family members have witnessed inappropriate behavior, ask them to write statements that you can use in your case. Just make sure these sources are reliable, and the information they give is relevant and legally okay to use.

Now, let's talk about voice and video recordings. These can be compelling tools, but there are essential rules to follow. The laws about recording conversations can vary a lot from state to state. Some states require you to inform both parties that you're recording them, while others only need one person's consent. This means you have to be super careful and know the laws in your state before you start recording. Recording someone without prior consent might be inadmissible in court and get you into legal trouble.

However, there are exceptions to these rules, especially in dangerous situations. If you are in immediate danger or if there is a threat of violence, some states have provisions that allow you to record without consent. Always consult a legal professional to understand what is permissible in your situation. For instance, if your ex is verbally abusive during a custody exchange and you fear for your safety, having that on tape can be strong evidence. Just remember, these recordings should be factual and straightforward. Don't try to provoke your ex into saying something incriminating; that could backfire.

Keeping this documentation safe is just as important as gathering it. Digital backups on secure, encrypted drives or cloud storage are a must. Physical copies should be stored securely, like a locked, fire-proof file cabinet or safe. This way, your records are secure from tampering or accidental loss, and you can access them whenever you need, whether for a lawyer's meeting or a court date.

Consider organizing your documents so they are easy to access and reference. Create folders for different types of evidence, such as communications, financial records, and character references. This organization can help you quickly find what you need when preparing for court.

Here's a simple sample for documenting interactions with your ex:

Date: July 28, 2024

Time: 3:45 PM

Interaction: Phone Call

Duration: 15 minutes

Summary of Interaction:

Today, [Ex] called to discuss the upcoming school event. The conversation started calmly, with us agreeing on the time and place for drop-off. However, [Ex] became upset when I mentioned I would take the kids to the event. They accused me of trying to "hog" all the events despite agreeing that I would attend this one earlier. [Ex] raised their voice and insisted that they should have the final say on who attends. I calmly reminded them of our previous agreement and tried to refocus the conversation on the kids' needs. [Ex] continued to argue but eventually agreed to let me take them, although they seemed unhappy.

Notes:

- [Ex] attempted to change the previously agreed-upon plans.
- The tone became confrontational when discussing event attendance.
- There is no resolution on how we will handle future events.

This format helps you keep track of your interactions, including any changes in agreements, disputes, and the overall tone of the conversations. It's important to be objective and detailed, sticking to the facts instead of emotions. You can attach screenshots, text messages, photos, or emails to the document for easy access and reference.

Creating a summarized spreadsheet provides a streamlined and organized way to document interactions with your ex. It allows you to maintain a clear and chronological record of every communication, making it easy to track patterns, follow up on unresolved issues, and provide evidence if needed. Summarizing each interaction lets you quickly recall the main points without sifting through lengthy conversations. The links to detailed records ensure that all relevant information is easily accessible without cluttering the summary view. This system helps you stay organized and minimizes the emotional toll of revisiting past interactions, as you can focus on the facts rather than reliving the entire experience. Essentially, this spreadsheet is a practical tool for managing co-parenting communication, ensuring you have a reliable reference point for legal or personal needs.

Sample Spreadsheet Layout

Date	Time	Type of Interaction	Brief Summary	Link to Detailed Record
07/28/2024	3:45 PM	Phone Call	Discussed upcoming school event, disagreement on attendance	Detailed Record
07/25/2024	1:30 PM	Email	Talked about summer vacation plans, agreement reached	Detailed Record
07/22/2024	10:00 AM	In-Person	Dropped kids off, short conversation about schoolwork	Detailed Record
07/18/2024	6:00 PM	Text Message	Requested change in visitation schedule, denied	Detailed Record

When you keep these detailed records, it helps paint a clear picture of your ex's behavior. Courts love specifics. Instead of saying, "My ex is unreliable," you can show them exactly how often your ex has missed visits or failed to communicate important information. It turns your words into facts that are hard to argue with.

Understanding what makes evidence admissible in court is another crucial step. Legal standards for admissible evidence can vary, but generally, your documentation must be relevant to your case, obtained legally, and verified for authenticity. Talk to your lawyer to ensure your documentation meets these criteria and effectively supports your claims in legal settings.

Thanks to technology, documenting interactions has become more accessible. There are apps and software designed explicitly for co-parenting. These tools let you log communications, share calendars, and document expenses related to your children. They help organize your evidence; courts often accept them because they have time stamps. Digital records can be particularly persuasive in court because they're clear, comprehensive, and reliable.

Third-party communication services can make co-parenting easier by reducing the need for direct contact. There are various apps and platforms designed to manage co-parenting communications. Apps like OurFamilyWizard or Talking Parents can help you manage communications and schedules, document interactions, and make them easily accessible. These tools allow you to exchange information about schedules, health updates, and school matters without direct interaction. Features like message encryption, read receipts and exportable logs can be very helpful. They help maintain a clear record of communications, which can be valuable in future legal or mediation sessions. Using these platforms minimizes conflict and creates a verifiable trail of your interactions.

When it's time to present your documentation in court, preparation is vital. Organize your evidence clearly and logically to tell a compelling story. Show not just isolated incidents but a pattern of behavior that has affected your and your children's lives. Your lawyer can help select the most critical pieces of evidence and advise on how to present them effectively. This might include creating summaries, using visuals like charts or timelines, or preparing briefs highlighting key evidence and their relevance to your case.

Your detailed documentation can make a huge difference in your legal battle. It gives you the clarity needed to counteract a narcissist's manipulations and ensures that your voice, grounded in truth and supported by evidence, is heard loud and clear. This strengthens your case and shows your commitment to protecting your rights and children's well-being amidst the ongoing challenges.

2.4 Child Support and Financial Disputes

Child support is there to make sure your kids have everything they need—like food, clothes, school supplies, and trips to the doctor. But if your ex is a narcissist, they might try to mess with the system to make things more complicated for you. They might lie about how much money they make or pretend to have more debts than they do. They may use financial manipulation tactics and dodge their financial responsibilities.

Now, let's dive into financial manipulation. This is a sneaky tactic some narcissists use to control or punish their exes. Imagine this: your ex starts delaying or even completely stopping child support payments just to get under your skin. It's like they're playing a twisted game with your finances. Or maybe they go all out and spoil the kids with gifts when they're with them, making you seem like the "bad" parent who can't keep up.

Narcissists might also try to misinterpret court orders to dodge their financial duties. They could argue that they don't have to pay for your child's piano lessons or school field trips, even if the court said they do. They'll twist and turn the rules to fit their needs, ignoring what's written in black and white. This constant battle can be exhausting. Having every detail about child custody and support in the court order is super important. This way, you've got legal backing if they try to skip out on their responsibilities. Here's a tip: always keep a copy of the court order nearby. You can refer to the document whenever your ex tries to pull a fast one and stand your ground.

THREE

Effective Communication Techniques

C ommunicating with a narcissist, especially when you're co-parenting, can feel like walking through a minefield. Almost every word you say can trigger an explosive reaction, and you never know when the next outburst will happen. It's like trying to keep peace in a storm. But don't worry, there are ways to handle this. It's all about understanding how they tick and learning how to respond in a way that keeps things calm and straightforward for your kids.

One of the most important things to remember is to keep your communications in writing. Texts, emails, even written notes—these are your friends. Avoid phone calls or in-person conversations if you can. Written communication provides a record of what you said. It's like having a backup in case things get twisted later. For instance, if you agree on something about the kids' schedule, having it in writing means you can refer back to it if your ex tries to change the story.

Let's say your ex sends a snarky message about you being late for a pickup. Instead of firing back or calling to argue, you calmly write a response like, "I arrived at 4:30 PM as scheduled." There is no drama, just facts. This helps calm the situation and shows you're sticking to the truth. Plus, it's all in black and white if you need to show it later.

3.1 Basic Principles

First, let's discuss a narcissist's typical communication patterns. Narcissists love dominating conversations, twisting words, and manipulating the story to fit their narrative. They might gaslight, project, or twist your words, all to keep control. Recognizing these tactics is your first step. It helps you stay one step ahead and keep the conversation on track.

Being clear and direct is your best weapon. Use simple, factual language to leave little room for misinterpretation. Keep it short and to the point, avoiding any emotional flair that your ex might use against you. For example, if you need to inform them about a school event, just say, "There is a parent-teacher meeting on Friday at 3 PM." There is no need to dive into reasons or frustrations. This keeps the focus on the facts and reduces the chance of emotional flare-ups.

Staying emotionally neutral is challenging but vital. Think of it like being a diplomat: calm, polite, and composed. By not showing your emotions, you prevent the narcissist from gaining emotional leverage. It's like playing chess, where you calculate every move and remain emotion-free. Keep your tone steady and your posture relaxed to help de-escalate potential conflicts.

Another great strategy is to plan your responses ahead of time. Before you even open that email or text from your ex, take a deep breath and remind yourself to stay calm. Think about how you can respond in a way that doesn't add fuel to the fire. Sometimes, it helps to draft your reply and wait a few minutes or even overnight before sending it. This gives you time to ensure your message is as calm and straightforward as possible.

Lastly, stick to the facts. Use specific details, like dates and times, to ensure clear and precise communication. Avoid vague statements that they can twist. For example, instead of saying, "You're so unreliable," try, "Today at 9 AM, the school nurse called and asked me to pick up our sick child. They tried to reach you but couldn't get through, so I handled the pickup at 9:45 AM. I then tried to drop the kids off at your place, but you were still unreachable. You can pick up the child from my residence at your convenience." Providing detailed information like this makes it harder for them to twist your words and keeps the focus on clear, factual communication.

Case Study: Communicating in High-Conflict Situations

Let's examine Maria's story to see how these communication techniques work. Maria is a mom trying to co-parent with her narcissistic ex. As you can imagine, this isn't easy. Her ex loves to use emotional accusations to mess up their conversations about the kids. But Maria found a way to handle it better by changing how she communicated.

Keeping it Factual

Once, during a discussion about their son Tim's school needs, her ex began accusing her of being too controlling, launching into a rant about how she always had to have things her way and never listened to his input. He continued, saying that she micromanaged every little aspect of Tim's life and made him feel like he had no say in his son's upbringing. Instead of getting defensive or upset, Maria stayed calm and focused on the facts. She calmly responded, "I'm focused on discussing Tim's need for tutoring in math, which we agreed he requires. Let's finalize the tutoring schedule." This kept the conversation on track and showed her ex that his outbursts wouldn't sway her.

This simple, factual response did wonders. It took the conversation away from the personal attack and brought it back to the real issue —Tim's tutoring. By doing this, Maria was able to steer the conversation back on track and reduce the chances of it turning into a heated argument.

Your goal when communicating with your ex isn't to win. Focus on protecting your and your kids' interests. This mindset shift is crucial. Instead of seeing conversations as battles to win, view them as opportunities to keep things clear and centered on what truly matters—the well-being of your children. By staying calm, sticking to the facts, and not getting pulled into emotional traps, you can make your interactions with your narcissistic ex more manageable and focused. This approach takes practice, especially staying calm when things get heated. But with time, you'll find it easier to keep calm and handle conversations effectively.

Practical Steps

Here's how you can do it:

1. **Stay Calm**: No matter how heated things get, keep your cool.
2. **Be Direct**: Use clear and straightforward language. Avoid getting emotional.
3. **Stick to the Facts**: Mention specific dates, times, and details.
4. **Focus on the Kids**: Always bring the conversation back to what's best for your children.

3.2 The Grey Rock Method

When dealing with a narcissistic ex, especially in co-parenting, you might find yourself constantly on edge, waiting for the next emotional ambush. That's where the Grey Rock Method comes in handy. This technique involves making yourself as bland and unemotional as a grey rock. It sounds weird, but it's surprisingly effective.

Imagine dealing with a narcissistic ex who loves drama and emotional reactions. They live for those moments when they can push your buttons and watch you explode. But what if you could be as uninteresting as a grey rock? That's the idea here. The Grey Rock Method is about being as dull and unresponsive as possible when interacting with a narcissist. It means not showing big emotions like anger, frustration, or excitement. Think about the last time your ex said something to get under your skin. Maybe they criticized your parenting or made a snide comment about something personal. Instead of reacting with anger or hurt, you stay calm and neutral. You respond with plain, factual statements.

Why does this work? Because narcissists need emotional fuel. They thrive on your reactions. When you don't give them that fuel, they lose interest. It's like trying to start a fire with wet wood—it just doesn't catch. So, if your ex says, "You're always late picking up the kids," instead of getting defensive or upset, you simply say, "I arrived at 4:30 PM as scheduled." No drama, no emotion, just facts. The key is to keep your responses simple and direct. Don't give them any extra information they can twist or use against you. If they ask about something personal, give short, factual answers. If they try to start an argument, don't engage. Just stick to the facts and keep your emotions out of it.

Practicing the Grey Rock Method takes time and patience. Staying calm and neutral is difficult when someone tries to provoke you. But with practice, it becomes more natural. Start by preparing yourself before interactions. Remind yourself to stay calm and stick to the facts. If you feel yourself getting emotional, take a deep breath and refocus. Let's look at a real-life example. Imagine your ex sends you a text saying, "You never help with the kids' schoolwork. I'm doing everything on my own!" Instead of responding with frustration or explaining all the times you've helped, you say, "I helped the kids with their homework on Monday and Wednesday this week." That's it. There is no defense, no emotion, just facts. The benefits of the Grey Rock Method are huge. First, it helps you avoid unnecessary conflict. By not reacting emotionally, you take away the narcissist's power to provoke you. Second, it protects your emotional well-being.

The biggest perk of the Grey Rock Method is that it helps prevent arguments. When you don't react emotionally, there's nothing for the narcissist to grab onto. They often lose interest and move on.

This means fewer fights and less stress for you. Plus, it helps you keep your emotional health in check by staying out of their manipulative games.

Of course, nothing is perfect. Sometimes, if the narcissist doesn't get the reaction they want, they might try even harder to provoke you. They might start acting out more or try new ways to get under your skin. This can be tough. Imagine your ex suddenly getting louder, meaner, or more persistent to make you react. They might bring up old arguments, say hurtful things, or even try to use the kids against you. It can feel like you're staying calm because they're heating up. But this is where you must be strong and stick to your grey rock approach. Remember, they're looking for that emotional reaction; if you don't give it to them, they'll eventually lose interest.

3.3 False Accusations

Let's talk about something nobody wants to deal with, but sometimes it happens – false accusations from your ex. It's one of those things that can make your heart race and your mind spin, especially when it pops up on a parenting app. So, what do you do when facing these kinds of accusations? Let's break it down in a way that's easy to handle.

First things first, don't panic. I know it's easier said than done but take a deep breath. Remember, jumping to defend yourself immediately can sometimes make things worse. So, before you do anything, just take a moment to calm down. Go for a walk, have a cup of tea, or do something that helps you relax.

Read through the accusations carefully. This isn't the time to skim – you must understand the claims. Sometimes, the allegations might be vague or sound like a big misunderstanding. Knowing what you're dealing with helps you decide how to respond.

Start tracking everything. Screenshot the messages, write down dates, and note any important details. Think of this like keeping a journal—it's just about recording what's happening so you can reflect on it if necessary.

Not every accusation needs a response. If the accusation is minor or ridiculous, it is best to ignore it. Sometimes, responding can give the accusation more attention than it deserves. But you should reply if the accusation is severe or could affect your relationship with your kids.

When you do decide to respond, keep it short, sweet, and to the point. Imagine you're explaining the situation to a friend – you don't need to write an essay. Just stick to the facts and stay calm. Here's a little example:

"Hey, I saw your message about [accusation]. I want to clarify things. [Briefly explain your side of the story]."

Notice how it's straightforward and doesn't get into a fight? That's the goal – clear communication without adding fuel to the fire.

Responding with a counteraccusation is tempting, but try to resist. Focus on what's best for your kids and how you can move forward. It's not about winning an argument; it's about keeping things positive for everyone involved.

If false accusations keep coming or get out of hand, it might be time to get help. Talking to a mediator can be helpful. They're like a neutral party who can help you both communicate better. And if things get dire, don't hesitate to talk to your attorney. They can give you advice on what steps to take next.

Keep all your communication on the parenting app, even if things get tough. It creates a clear record of everything said, which can be vital if you need to show it to a mediator or in court.

3.4 Scripts

Communication with a narcissistic ex can be stressful. Every word you say has to be carefully chosen to keep things smooth and focused on the kids' best interests. Having some pre-written scripts can be a huge help. These scripts guide you through common scenarios, helping you stay clear, concise, and free from unnecessary conflict. They let you get your point across effectively while avoiding manipulative tactics.

Daily Communication

Let's start with daily communication about the kids' schedules, health, and school matters. The key here is to be brief and precise. When you keep it simple, there's less chance for things to get twisted or turn into an argument. Here are some examples to help you navigate different scenarios.

Example 1: School Schedule Changes

Imagine you need to tell your ex about a change in the school schedule. Your message could be, "Just to update you, the school has shifted the PTA meeting to next Thursday at 3 PM. I plan to attend and will share any significant updates with you." This script is straightforward and informative. It sticks to the facts and avoids opening any avenues for unnecessary debate.

Example 2: Health Updates

Suppose your child has a doctor's appointment, and you must inform your ex. You might say, "Our child has a check-up with Dr. Smith on Monday at 2 PM. I will take them and let you know if there are any important updates." This keeps the communication focused on the essential details without inviting any unnecessary comments or arguments.

Example 3: School Projects or Homework

If your child has a big school project or needs help with homework, you could say, "Just wanted to let you know, our child has a science project due next Friday. I will help them gather materials and start the project this weekend." By sticking to the facts and not delving into how much time and effort it will take, you keep the message clear and direct.

Example 4: Extracurricular Activities

When informing your ex about an extracurricular activity, your message might be, "Our child has soccer practice every Tuesday and Thursday at 4 PM. I will take them this week." This provides all the necessary information about the schedule without inviting further discussion or conflict.

Example 5: Medication and Health Care

For updates on your child's medication or health care, you could write, "The doctor prescribed a new medication for our child, which they need to take twice daily. I will handle the morning dose. Please ensure they take the evening dose." This ensures parents are informed and involved in the child's health care without adding emotional weight to the message.

Example 6: Sharing School Performance

When updating your ex on the child's school performance, you might say, "Our child received their report card today. They did well in most subjects but need some help with math. I have scheduled a meeting with their teacher for next Wednesday at 10 AM." This gives a clear update and shows steps you take without opening the door to criticism or blame.

Custody or Visitation Changes

Talking about changes in custody or visitation schedules can be tricky when co-parenting with a difficult ex. These talks often become arguments, so handling them carefully is super important. Focus on clear communication instead of getting into fights. Make changes to custody or visitation as a last resort. The main goal is to ensure everything is in your kids' best interest. Let's look at some examples to help you manage these tough conversations.

Example 1: Vacation Planning

You could approach it like this: "I'm planning a vacation for the kids during the summer break. The trip will be from June 10th to June 17th. We will be flying out on June 10th with Flight 123, departing at 9 AM and returning on June 17th with Flight 456, arriving at 4

PM." Presenting the information clearly and with all the details keeps the communication straightforward and positive.

Example 2: Addressing Overlaps with Special Events

Suppose a special event like a family reunion, funeral, or wedding conflicts with the visitation schedule. In that case, you might say, "There's a family reunion coming up on a weekend that falls during your parenting time. The kids need to attend. Could we discuss a way to adjust the schedule just for that weekend?" This way, you're showing respect for the existing schedule while highlighting the importance of the event.

Parenting Decisions

Handling disagreements over parenting decisions can be challenging, especially with a narcissistic ex. It's important to stand your ground but also be diplomatic. You don't want to stir up more trouble, but you must ensure your kids are cared for properly. Here's how you can approach these tricky conversations.

Example 1: How to disagree on an Issue

If you disagree with a parenting decision proposed by your ex, you could say, "Hey, I get where you're coming from, but I'm worried about how this affects the kids and our parenting plan. Can we look at other options that might work for both of us?" This script acknowledges their view (which is crucial with narcissists who seek validation) but firmly expresses your concerns and steers towards a compromise.

Example 2: Doctor Recommended Procedure

Imagine the doctor recommends a medical procedure for your child, but your ex disagrees. You might say, "Hey, I get your worries about the procedure, but the doctor thinks it's important for our kid's health. Can we discuss why the doctor recommends it and see how we can address your concerns while following their advice?"

This shows you respect their worries but emphasizes the importance of following medical advice.

Example 3: Summer Camp

If your ex wants to send the kids to a summer camp you're uncomfortable with, you could say, "Hey, I know you think summer camp would be awesome for the kids, but I'm worried about the camp's safety and how far it is from home. Can we check out some closer camps with good safety records instead?" This way, you acknowledge their idea while ensuring the kids' safety and comfort.

Example 4: School Program

If the school recommends your child for a selective program, but your ex disagrees, you could say, "Hey, I know you're worried about our kid joining the program, but their teachers think it will help their education and growth. Can we discuss your concerns and see if there's a way to address them while giving our kid this chance?" This emphasizes the benefits for the child while showing a willingness to address any worries your ex might have.

Handling Emergency Situations

When it comes to emergencies, the main thing to remember is to keep the focus on your child's welfare. You need to be direct and clear, with no room for misunderstandings. Here are some ways to handle different emergency scenarios with your narcissistic ex.

Example 1: High Fever

Imagine your child suddenly develops a high fever and needs immediate medical attention. You might say, "Our child has a high fever, and I think we should see a doctor immediately. I plan to take them to urgent care unless you have any objections or other suggestions. Please let me know immediately." This message is straightforward and action-oriented. It shows that you're taking the situation seriously and inviting your ex to contribute without leaving room for delay.

Example 2: Injury at School

Suppose your child gets injured at school and needs to go to the hospital. You could say, "Our child had an accident at school and needs to go to the hospital. I'm taking them to the emergency room now. I'll keep you updated on their condition. If you have any concerns or other ideas, please let me know as soon as possible." This way, you inform them of the situation and your immediate actions and leave space for their input.

Example 3: Allergic Reaction

If your child has an allergic reaction and needs quick intervention, you might say, "Our child is having an allergic reaction, and I'm taking them to the nearest clinic immediately. I'll keep you posted on their condition. Let me know if you have any other advice or suggestions." This ensures that your ex is informed and can provide input, but it's clear that you are handling the emergency.

Remember, the goal isn't to win an argument but to protect your peace and keep things stable for your kids. It's tough, but you can get better at it with practice. Keep using these techniques; over time, they'll become second nature. You'll handle those tricky interactions with more confidence and less stress.

Here's a bonus tip: Using AI to help write a message to your ex can be super helpful, especially when you need a specific tone. Whether you want to sound calm, professional, friendly, casual, or firm but fair, AI can help you get it right. Just tell the AI about the situation and how you want to come across, and it will help you craft a clear message that reduces misunderstandings. Plus, using AI can help take your emotions out of the equation, ensuring your message stays focused and doesn't get influenced by how you're feeling. This makes communication smoother and less stressful, which is excellent for keeping things peaceful and focused on what's best for your kids.

3.5 Gaslighting

Gaslighting is a sneaky way for someone to make you doubt your memories and feelings. Recognizing when this is happening to you is essential. Your ex might say things like, "I never said that," or, "You're remembering it wrong," even when you know what happened. These little tricks can make you start questioning your sanity.

Imagine discussing holiday plans, and your ex insists you never agreed on something you both talked about. They might say, "We never said I'd have the kids for Christmas. You must be imagining things." This can leave you feeling confused and unsure of yourself. However, the first step in fighting back is to recognize this pattern. When you notice these tactics, it signals that your ex is trying to mess with your mind.

Once you spot gaslighting, the next step is to respond with solid proof. If your ex tries to deny something you remember clearly, you can say, "I have an email from you dated December 1st where you agreed to this plan." Using specific, documented evidence helps you stand firm in your reality and makes it harder for your ex to twist the truth. It's like shining a flashlight in a dark room—suddenly, everything becomes more evident. This is one of the many reasons why thorough documentation is necessary.

Dealing with gaslighting can take a toll on your emotions. You might start feeling anxious or unsure of yourself. It's so important to get support from outside. Talking to a therapist who understands narcissistic abuse can give you strategies to deal with these tactics and help you rebuild your confidence. Joining support groups, whether online or in person, can also be helpful. These groups remind you that you're not alone and provide a space to share stories and advice with others who understand what you're going through.

Handling gaslighting requires staying alert, using clear communication, and getting solid emotional support. By learning to spot the signs, responding with evidence, keeping detailed records, and seeking help, you can protect yourself from the confusing effects of gaslighting. This approach helps you ensure others hear your voice and recognize your truth. It's not just about dealing with your ex but also about rebuilding your own confidence and emotional health. This is crucial as you navigate the ups and downs of co-parenting.

3.6 Mediation

Mediation can provide a structured environment where you can address disputes without getting too emotional. It's beneficial when direct communication breaks down or becomes too heated. A professional mediator guides the conversation, ensuring both sides speak and find practical solutions. Mediation can be an excellent tool for resolving specific issues like custody arrangements, visitation schedules, or other parenting problems without all the emotional baggage.

Selecting the right mediator is very important. You want someone who has experience with high-conflict personalities or specializes in family disputes involving narcissism. These mediators know how to handle manipulation and can spot tactics used to derail discussions. They focus on what's best for the children and help steer the conversation back on track if it goes off course. You can find good mediators through local mediation centers or family law attorneys. It is a good idea to interview a few mediators to ensure they have the right experience and approach for your needs. Getting recommendations from people who have used mediators is also a great idea. They can suggest someone good or tell you who to avoid.

Going to mediation takes more than just showing up. You need to prepare carefully. Start by gathering all relevant documents and evidence that support your position or clarify your concerns. This might include communication logs, visitation records, or documentation of your child's needs and expenses. Organize your thoughts and concerns into a clear list of discussion points, prioritizing them by importance. This preparation helps you stay focused and ensures you cover all critical issues without getting sidetracked by your ex's tactics. Present your points calmly during mediation and listen actively to the mediator and your ex's responses. Remember, the goal isn't to win but to find workable solutions for your children.

FOUR

Setting and Maintaining Boundaries

I magine trying to assemble a puzzle without the picture on the box. Knowing where each piece fits would be hard without a clear image, and you might end up with a jumbled mess. This is just like having boundaries in your life, especially when you're dealing with a problematic ex-partner. One wrong word can cause things to get messy quickly. Boundaries help you know where healthy interactions stop, and toxic ones begin. They are essential for keeping you emotionally, mentally, and physically healthy. This chapter is all about understanding these boundaries, why they matter, the challenges you'll face in maintaining them, and how they can improve your life and co-parenting experience.

A boundary is something you decide and enforce to protect your well-being. It's not about controlling what your ex does but about how you will respond to their actions. For example, if you set a boundary that you won't answer calls after 8 PM, it's not about making your ex stop calling; it's about choosing not to pick up the phone after that time. Boundaries are all about what you will do to care for yourself, no matter what your ex does.

4.1 The Importance of Boundaries

Boundaries are like invisible fences that protect your self-esteem and personal integrity. These boundaries show what you value, your limits, and what kinds of interactions you can accept. In a toxic relationship, boundaries are your shield. They help keep your mind peaceful, your emotions stable, and your personal space safe.

For example, you might decide not to talk to your ex unless it's about your kids. Or, you might rule that you won't answer calls or texts outside of specific times. This way, you can keep the chaos and manipulation to a minimum, focusing instead on things that make you happy and fulfilled. By saying, "I won't tolerate any mean comments during our talks," you create a more respectful and manageable environment.

Narcissists often see boundaries as challenges and might react angrily or coldly. They might try to break these boundaries repeatedly, hoping you'll give up and return to the old ways where they had more control. These reactions can make you feel disheartened and wonder if it's worth it. However, these challenges show just how vital firm boundaries are.

Over time, maintaining these boundaries does more than reduce stress and keep you emotionally stable. It helps you build self-respect and shows your needs and feelings are valid. This self-respect can improve all your relationships, making it easier for you to recognize and demand healthy interactions. In co-parenting, firm boundaries help you better deal with your ex and show your kids that respect and self-care are essential to any relationship.

To help you set and keep these boundaries, try a boundary-mapping exercise. Start by thinking about where your boundaries are currently not respected. Write these down. Then, imagine what a healthy boundary would look like in each situation. For instance, if you often end up in pointless arguments about parenting, a boundary might be to walk away from any conversation that turns into criticism or blame. After creating your list, consider practical steps to set these boundaries and plan your response when someone tests them. This exercise helps you see where you need boundaries and empowers you to start setting them proactively.

Setting and keeping effective boundaries with a narcissistic ex is essential for navigating the challenges of co-parenting. It takes clarity, consistency, and courage. By defining and enforcing these boundaries, you protect your emotional and mental health, improve your relationships, and create a stable and healthy environment for your children. As you continue to build and reinforce these boundaries, remember how important they are—not just for managing your relationship with your ex but as a foundation for your well-being and growth.

4.2 Practical Steps to Establish Firm Boundaries

We've covered why boundaries matter, so now, let's focus on how actually to establish them. Setting boundaries may feel daunting initially, but it's all about figuring out what suits you best and staying consistent. Whether you're already comfortable with setting limits or this is new ground for you, we have some practical steps to guide you. Let's break it down step by step.

First, take a moment to think about your past interactions with your ex. Were there times when you felt overwhelmed, disrespected, or manipulated? These feelings are important clues about where you need to set boundaries. Setting boundaries isn't just about saying "no" to certain things; it's about creating a safe and respectful space for yourself.

Start by identifying specific situations that made you uncomfortable. For example, you noticed that discussions with your ex often lead to arguments. In this case, a boundary could be to minimize conversations to just ones about the kids. This helps keep your interactions focused and prevents them from drifting into personal attacks or manipulative areas.

If multiple harassing calls from your ex left you anxious, that's another sign you need a boundary. You might decide to only talk during specific hours, like 6 PM and 8 PM. This way, you can avoid those stressful interactions.

Additionally, if you notice that face-to-face interactions during child exchanges often lead to tension and conflict, you can set a boundary only to do curbside exchanges. This means you stay in your car, and your ex stays in theirs, minimizing direct contact and reducing the chance of conflict. This boundary can help make the exchange process smoother and less stressful for you and your kids.

Once you know what boundaries you need, the next step is communicating them to your ex. You need to do this in a straightforward, no-nonsense way. This isn't about asking for permission—it's about letting them know how things will work from now on. For instance, you could say, "I will only discuss matters directly related to the kids' health and schooling. Focusing on these topics will help us stay on track and avoid unrelated discussions." Notice how this is a statement, not a request. You're laying down the law on how things will be moving forward.

Make sure your boundaries are clearly defined. Vague boundaries can be misunderstood or ignored. Be specific about what behavior is okay and what isn't, and what will happen if someone crosses your boundary. For example, you might say that any communication outside the set hours won't get an immediate response or that using disrespectful language will end the conversation. Being specific helps prevent misunderstandings and makes it easier to stick to your boundaries.

4.3 Enforcing Boundaries Without Escalation

Having boundaries is one thing, but the real challenge comes with enforcing them. Narcissists are known for repeatedly testing limits, looking for any wiggle room they can exploit. That's why consistency is essential. Here's how you can enforce your boundaries without making things worse.

When you need to enforce a boundary, stay calm. If your ex tries to talk to you in person, avoid getting into a confrontation. Instead, respond simply like, "Let's keep our communication on the parenting app." This keeps things clear without sparking an argument.

Using neutral language is critical. Instead of saying, "You always call too late and ruin my evening," try, "I'll be available for calls between 6 - 8 PM. Let's talk tomorrow during those hours." This way, you're clearly stating your boundary without giving them a chance to get defensive or angry.

It's important not to let your emotions take over during these interactions. If your ex sees they can upset you, they might keep pushing your buttons. Practice staying calm by taking deep breaths, pausing to think before you speak, or stepping away from the conversation if you feel yourself getting upset.

Enforcing boundaries with a narcissistic ex can feel like walking through a minefield. One wrong move can lead to a big fight. But with the right strategies, you can keep things under control. Be non-confrontational, use neutral language, stay emotionally detached, and know when to ask for help. These steps will help you maintain your boundaries without escalating the situation.

By consistently doing this, you show that you're serious about your boundaries. This protects your emotional and physical health and helps create a more respectful and peaceful co-parenting relationship. You show that while you want to work together for the kids, you won't compromise on respect and safety.

Maintaining boundaries requires a mix of firmness and flexibility. Be firm in your commitment to your boundaries but flexible in handling situations as they arise. Every interaction is unique, and while your boundaries should stay consistent, how you enforce them might need to adapt depending on the context. This adaptive approach ensures that you respond appropriately to different situations without compromising your established limits.

Flexibility means being able to adapt to different situations while still respecting your boundaries. Life is unpredictable; sometimes, you may need to adjust your approach. For instance, if an emergency involves your child, you might need to respond outside your usual communication hours. This doesn't mean you have broken your boundary; it simply means you are flexible enough to handle urgent matters appropriately.

Sometimes, your ex might not respect your boundaries at all. If they keep breaking agreements that affect your safety or well-being, it might be time to get help. This could mean talking to a lawyer, getting a mediator to help with new agreements, or even involving the police if things get serious.

For instance, if your ex keeps coming to your house without an invitation or breaks a restraining order, keeping you and your kids safe is critical. In these cases, don't hesitate to call the authorities. It's essential to take action to protect yourself and your family.

4.4 Handling Boundary Violations Gracefully

Setting boundaries with a narcissistic ex can be challenging. When you draw a line, it's important to recognize when someone crosses it. Staying alert to these violations helps you respond before things get out of hand. For example, if your ex starts showing up at your house unannounced or tries to change plans at the last minute without consulting you, it's time to take action.

First, it's crucial to recognize boundary violations early on to maintain your limits. For example, your ex might start by sending text messages late at night, even when you've asked for communication to happen only during certain hours. Or they might frequently "forget" to return the kids' belongings after a visit. By noticing these subtle boundary pushes early on, you can address them before they escalate into more significant issues.

When someone crosses your boundaries, it's normal to feel upset. However, reacting in anger can escalate the situation. Instead, take a moment to calm down and consider your response. For example, if your ex starts discussing personal matters in front of the kids when you've agreed to keep such conversations private, you can calmly say, "We've agreed not to discuss these topics in front of the children. Let's save this conversation for another time." This way, you assert your boundary without creating additional tension.

Documenting boundary violations is necessary. Write down each incident with details like date, time, what happened, and how you responded. This isn't just for your records; it can be helpful if you need to discuss these issues in mediation or therapy. Having a log shows a pattern of behavior that can support your case if you need to take further action.

After someone crosses a boundary, it's important to reset it. Let your ex know the boundary and what will happen if it's crossed again. For example, if your ex makes a disrespectful comment, you might say, "Respect is important when we talk. If the rude comments continue, we'll limit communication only through texts." This makes your expectations clear and sets consequences for future violations.

Use techniques like maintaining a neutral tone and avoiding defensive arguments to keep things from escalating. If a conversation gets heated, ending it and returning to it later is okay. This helps keep interactions calm and productive, showing you're committed to maintaining a peaceful co-parenting relationship.

Setting boundaries isn't just about keeping things peaceful—it's about taking back control and protecting yourself. Clear, specific, and consistent boundaries help create a respectful and manageable co-parenting situation. This helps you and benefits your children, reducing stress and conflict and creating a healthier environment for everyone.

By following these steps, you can set and maintain firm boundaries with your narcissistic ex-partner, improving your interactions and helping you feel more in control and less stressed.

4.5 Teaching Your Children About Boundaries

Teaching your children about boundaries is a powerful way to help them grow strong and confident. Here's how you can do it in a way that's easy for them to understand and apply.

Kids learn a lot by watching us. If they see you setting and keeping clear boundaries, they'll understand it's okay to have limits. For example, if you tell your ex that personal life topics are off-limits, your kids see you respecting yourself. This shows them it's also important to protect their space and feelings.

Start with simple lessons for younger kids, like teaching them to knock before entering a room. This helps them understand physical boundaries. As they get older, talk about respecting others' feelings and opinions. For teenagers, discuss more complex boundaries, like what's appropriate to share online. This helps them navigate friendships and social media safely.

Role-playing can be a fun and practical way to help kids practice setting boundaries. You can create scenarios where they might need to say "no" or stand up for themselves. For example, you could act out a situation where someone pressures them to keep a secret from you. Help them think about what they could say, like, "I don't keep secrets from my parents," and guide them through using an assertive tone. Explain why speaking up is important when they feel uncomfortable or something doesn't feel right. This practice can build their confidence and make them more prepared to handle real-life situations.

Another example could be practicing what to do if a friend tries to push them into doing something they don't want to, like playing a game they're uncomfortable with. You can role-play this scenario, helping them devise ways to say, "No, I don't want to play that game," or "I'd rather do something else." Discuss how walking away is okay if they feel pressured or their boundaries aren't respected. These exercises are about saying "no" and reinforcing that their feelings and choices matter. Rehearsing these scenarios teaches them to handle peer pressure and respect their boundaries.

If you notice the other parent belittling or ignoring your child's feelings or needs, address it with the child. For example, if you hear your child asking for some alone time and the other parent dismisses it, discuss it with your child afterward.

Talk to your child and let them know their feelings are important. Say, "I heard you asked for some alone time, and it's okay to need that. How can we make sure you get the privacy you need?" This shows your child that you respect their boundaries and that it's okay to have them.

After acknowledging their needs, talk about ways to help uphold these boundaries in the future. You could suggest, "Next time, let's set up a signal or a specific place you can go when you need some alone time. How does that sound?" This helps your child feel more in control and supported.

By consistently supporting your child's boundaries, you help them understand and respect their limits. They learn that their needs and feelings are valid, which builds their confidence. For example, if the other parent often interrupts when your child is doing homework, you can create a rule at your house that homework time is quiet time. This reinforces the importance of respecting personal space and time.

Supporting your child this way also helps reduce the negative impacts of disrespectful behavior from the other parent. Your support is a buffer if your child feels hurt or ignored by the other parent. They know they can always rely on you for understanding and respect. For example, if the other parent mocks their interests, you can counteract that negativity by showing extra support and enthusiasm. If your child loves to draw, ask to see their latest artwork and praise their creativity. Or, if they like to read, take an active interest in their favorite books. You could ask them to recommend a book or suggest a family book club where you read and discuss their favorite stories together.

Always encourage your child to talk to you about how they're feeling. Ask questions like, "How did you feel when that happened?" and listen carefully to their answers. Let them know it's okay to share anything with you, and you'll always be there to listen and help.

Show your child how to set and respect boundaries by doing the same in your own life. For example, if you need quiet time to work, tell them, "I need some quiet time to finish my work. Can we have some quiet time together?" This sets a good example and shows them it's okay to set limits.

4.6 Using the Law to Keep Boundaries in Place

The law can give you the authority and enforcement that personal boundaries or a court order alone can't always provide. By involving the legal system, you ensure your boundaries are recognized and backed by real consequences if violated. This might sound scary, but it's an important step to protect your peace of mind and your kids' well-being. Let's talk about how you can use the legal system to your advantage, understand the tools available, and take steps to uphold your boundaries. This process can help you create a safer, more structured environment free from the disruptions of a problematic co-parenting relationship.

A restraining order is a legal document from the court that stops a person from doing certain things, like contacting or coming near you. If your ex is harassing, threatening, or physically harming you, a restraining order can offer immediate protection. It's a legal way to keep them at a distance and prevent further harm.

First, head to your local courthouse and ask for the forms to request a restraining order. The court clerk can give you a packet of forms to fill out. The forms will ask you to explain why you need protection and describe any incidents. Be as clear and detailed as you can. This information helps the judge understand why you need the order.

After you complete the forms, turn them into the court clerk. They might ask you to wait while a judge reviews your request. Sometimes, you might need to go in front of the judge to explain your situation. This can feel nerve-wracking, but remember, the judge is there to help you. Speak honestly about what's been happening and why you feel unsafe.

You will receive a temporary restraining order if the judge grants your request. This order will tell your ex what they can't do, like coming near or contacting you. It's essential to always keep a copy of this order with you.

You will also get a date for a court hearing, usually within a few weeks. You and your ex can present your sides of the story at this hearing. It's a good idea to bring any evidence you have, like text messages, emails, or witness statements. The judge will then decide if they should extend the order.

Legal protection can help you feel safer and more in control. It's a big step, but you're doing it to protect yourself and your kids. Remember, you don't have to do this alone. Ask for help from friends, family, or a lawyer specializing in these cases.

Legal boundaries can help when dealing with a difficult ex. One of the most significant benefits is that they are enforceable. If your ex crosses these boundaries, they could face fines, community service, or jail time. Knowing there are real consequences gives you peace of mind. Plus, having these boundaries in place creates stability for your kids. They know what to expect and when which helps reduce anxiety and makes things more predictable.

If your ex breaks the rules, document everything. Keep records of emails, texts, and any incidents that happen. Let your lawyer know about any violations so they can guide you on what to do next, including possibly going back to court. Stay calm through all this, even though it can be stressful. Let the legal process work for you instead of reacting emotionally.

Making boundaries legal is a big step toward protecting yourself and your kids. It's all about creating a safer, more predictable environment where you can heal and move forward. By knowing the process and working with legal professionals, you can ensure your boundaries are respected and upheld.

FIVE

Protecting Children from Narcissistic Abuse

C o-parenting with a narcissist can create a challenging and unpredictable environment for your child. This chapter will help you understand and reduce the impact of emotional manipulation by a narcissistic parent. It's about noticing signs of distress, understanding why they happen, and taking steps to help your child thrive.

5.1 Recognizing Signs

It can be hard to notice the early signs of emotional manipulation in children, but catching them early is critical. Look out for minor changes that might show your child is struggling.

Behavioral changes are often the most noticeable signs. Your child might:

- Withdraw from social activities and family interactions.
- Show a sudden drop in academic performance.
- Start mimicking manipulative behaviors, like lying or using guilt to get what they want.

Children learn these behaviors to cope with their confusing and challenging world.

Emotionally, children might:

- Seem confused or distressed, especially about conflicting messages from each parent.
- Show mood swings, sudden tears, or anger that don't match the situation.

This emotional turbulence reflects their inner conflict as they try to reconcile the different parenting styles they encounter.

Narcissistic manipulation can hurt a child's self-esteem and how they see themselves. They might feel confused by mixed messages of praise and criticism, making them unsure about their worth. To help with this, it's important to:

- Do activities and have talks that make them feel good about themselves.
- Give them regular compliments and be emotionally supportive.
- Talk openly about their feelings and experiences.

These actions help them feel more confident and secure.

Paying attention to the interactions between your child and the narcissistic parent can give you insights into what might be affecting your child. Observe changes in your child's behavior before and after visits, and encourage open discussions about their feelings and experiences.

If your child seems upset or starts acting differently, it might be time to get help from a child psychologist or counselor. But remember, finding the right person for the job is essential. Not all professionals have the training to spot narcissistic abuse, so make sure you choose someone who understands what your child is going through.

Look for a psychologist or counselor who has experience with narcissistic abuse. You can ask other parents, check online reviews, or ask your child's doctor for recommendations. Finding someone who gets it can make a big difference.

Once you find the right professional, they can do a lot to help your child. They provide a safe space where your child can talk about their feelings. Your child might be scared or confused; having someone to listen and understand can greatly relieve them.

The counselor will help your child understand what they are feeling and why. This is the first step in dealing with those feelings healthily. The professional can also advise you on supporting your child at home. They might suggest activities that build your child's confidence or ways to handle difficult situations with the other parent.

It's not just about your child working with the counselor. You'll be involved, too. The counselor will likely meet with you to discuss what's happening and how you can help. This might include setting up a routine, being more patient, or finding new communication methods.

Remember, getting help is a big step towards making things better for your child. By working with the right professional, you can provide the support they need to feel safe and understood. This will help them grow stronger and more confident, even in a challenging situation.

5.2 Strategies to Protect the Children

Creating a loving and stable home is essential when you're co-parenting with someone who has narcissistic traits. It's not just about dealing with everyday stuff; it's about ensuring your kids feel safe, loved, and supported, even if the other parent is unpredictable or hurtful.

In this section, we'll examine practical ways to help your children cope with having a narcissistic parent. These tips will help you build a solid emotional base for your kids, give them tools to understand and handle challenging situations and ensure your home is a place of love and support. Doing this can help your children thrive, even with their challenges.

Let's examine specific strategies for protecting your children and creating a healthy, positive environment for them to grow up in.

Your home should be where your children feel comfortable expressing their feelings. It is essential to encourage open and honest conversations and show your kids that their feelings matter.

Try setting up a daily "feelings check-in" during dinner. This is a time when everyone can share something about their day. For example, you can start by saying, "Today was a good day because I finished my work early," or "I felt sad today because I missed my friend." This helps your children see that it's okay to talk about their feelings and that everyone has different emotions.

Create a cozy corner where your kids can relax and talk. This could be a living room corner with comfy cushions, blankets, and some of their artwork on the walls. Encourage them to use this space when they need a quiet moment or want to talk about something on their mind. You might say, "If you ever need a break or want to chat, you can always go to the cozy corner."

Let your children know that they can talk to you about anything. When they come to you with their feelings, listen without interrupting and show that you care about what they're saying. For example, if your child says, "I felt left out at school today," you can respond with, "I'm sorry you felt that way. Do you want to talk about what happened?"

Validate your children's feelings. Let them know that feeling sad, angry, happy, or anything in between is okay. If your child is upset, you can say, "It's okay to feel angry. Everyone gets angry sometimes. Let's talk about what made you feel this way."

In addition to daily check-ins, have regular one-on-one conversations with each child. This allows them to talk about anything bothering them without feeling rushed. Ask questions like, "How are you feeling about school?" or "Is there anything you want to discuss?"

Being present means giving your full attention when your child talks to you. Put away your phone, turn off the TV, and listen to them. This shows them that what they have to say is important to you.

Show empathy by putting yourself in their shoes. If your child is upset about a fight with a friend, you might say, "I understand you're upset. It can be tough when friends argue. Let's think about how we can make it better."

Building trust takes time, but it's worth it. Be consistent in your responses and show your children they can rely on you. If you promise to do something, make sure you follow through. This helps them feel safe and secure.

Children need predictability, especially when one parent is unpredictable. Establish a consistent routine for meals, homework, and bedtime. Stick to this schedule as much as possible, no matter what's happening with the other parent. For example, if your ex often breaks promises, always follow through on yours, even if it's just a tiny thing like a trip to the park. This helps your child feel secure and trust that you will always be there for them.

5.3 Teach Them About Manipulative Behaviors

Helping your children understand manipulative behaviors is essential. Start by having simple conversations about feelings and respect. Talk about how everyone has the right to feel safe and respected. For example, you might say, "Everyone's feelings are important, and it's okay to say how you feel."

As your children age, you can introduce ideas like manipulation and control. You don't have to mention the other parent directly. Instead, use stories from books or movies to explain these concepts. For instance, after watching a movie together, you could discuss a character who tried to get their way by making others feel guilty. You might say, "Did you see how that character tried to get what they wanted by making others feel bad? That's not a healthy way to treat people."

Role-playing is a great way to help your children practice recognizing and resisting manipulation. Create scenarios where they might need to say "no" or express their feelings. For example, you can pretend to be a friend who grabs something from their hand and says, "Give me that!" Teach them to respond firmly, "I don't like it when you take my things without asking. Please ask first." This practice helps them learn to stand up for themselves and set boundaries respectfully.

You can also practice situations where someone tries to make them feel guilty. Act out a scenario where someone says, "If you cared about me, you would do this for me." Teach your child to respond, "I care about you, but I don't feel comfortable doing that." This practice helps build their confidence and shows them they have the right to set boundaries.

Encourage your children to talk about their experiences and feelings. Ensure they know they can come to you if something feels wrong. For example, you might say, "If anyone ever makes you feel uncomfortable or tries to make you do something you don't want to, you can always tell me about it. I'm here to help."

Ask open-ended questions to get them talking. Instead of asking yes or no questions, try asking, "How did that make you feel?" or "What do you think about what happened?" This encourages them to share more and helps you understand their experiences better.

This isn't a one-time conversation. Keep talking with your children about these topics as they grow and face new situations. Check in with them regularly to see how they're doing and if they have any new concerns. Let them know that it's always okay to come to you with questions or problems.

By teaching your children about manipulative behaviors and giving them the tools to deal with them, you're helping them grow into strong, confident individuals. You're giving them the knowledge and support they need to navigate their relationships healthily and respectfully.

5.4 Discussing Narcissism with Children Appropriately

Talking to your kids about narcissism can be tricky, but it's essential to help them understand what's happening without making them feel scared or confused. Here's how you can explain these behaviors in a way that's easy for them to grasp and doesn't make them feel like they have to choose sides.

For younger kids, focus on explaining emotions and behaviors without using labels. You might say, "Sometimes, people feel sad or upset and might say things they don't mean. It can be confusing or hurtful." This helps them understand that people can act out when upset, and it's not always about them.

With older kids, you can go deeper. Explain that some people have a harder time understanding other people's feelings, making their actions seem selfish or uncaring. For example, you can say, "Some people find it hard to see things from other people's point of view. This can make them talk a lot about themselves or not listen well to others."

It's best to avoid labeling the other parent. Instead, focus on only describing their behaviors for kids to understand. For example, "Sometimes when your dad/mom says they'll do something and then changes their mind, that can be frustrating. If that happens, it's okay to feel disappointed. We can talk about it and figure out the best way to handle it together." This approach helps kids recognize and understand the behavior, encourages open communication, and reassures them that they don't have to deal with their feelings alone.

It's vital to reassure your kids that they are safe and loved no matter what. Ensure they know your home is a stable and loving place where they can always feel secure. For instance, after a confusing visit with the other parent, you might say, "I'm always here for you, and you can tell me anything. You are loved and safe here." You could also spend time together doing something comforting, like watching a favorite movie or cooking a special meal. These moments reinforce the idea that your home is a refuge where they can relax and be themselves. Remind them that no matter what happens, they have a constant source of love and support with you. They must understand that they don't have to hide their feelings or experiences and can rely on you for comfort and guidance. This reassurance helps build trust and emotional security, essential for their well-being.

Helping your kids understand what's going on can make them feel stronger and more in control. Have regular conversations where they can talk about their feelings and thoughts. Encourage them to ask questions and give honest, age-appropriate answers. This can help them feel less helpless and more resilient. For example, if they ask, "Why does Dad/Mom always talk about themselves?" you can respond, "Sometimes people don't realize they're doing it. It's important to remember it's not your fault."

Make sure your kids know they can talk to you about anything. Show interest in their thoughts and feelings, ask open-ended questions, and listen without interrupting. For example, you could ask, "How did you feel when that happened?" and then listen carefully to their response. This shows them that their feelings matter and that it's okay to express them.

Create an environment where your kids feel heard and supported. Spend time with them, show empathy, and validate their feelings. If your child says, "I felt ignored today," you can say, "I'm sorry you felt that way. It's important to feel listened to. Let's talk about it."

By talking about these things openly and with care, you help your children understand and deal with the challenges of having a narcissistic parent. This knowledge helps them stay emotionally healthy and build strong, positive relationships. Your support and understanding can make a big difference in how they navigate these experiences.

5.5 Building Kids' Self-Esteem

When helping your child develop a positive self-image, especially with a narcissistic co-parent, your role becomes super important. You need to undo the negative things they hear and fill them up with positivity, confidence, and self-worth. Here's how you can do that in a friendly, supportive, and fun way.

Positive affirmations are a great way to counteract the negative messages your child might get from a narcissistic parent. Think about phrases that make your child feel loved and valued for being themselves. For example, you can say, "I love you for who you are, not just for what you do," or "Your thoughts and feelings are important." Make these affirmations a part of your daily routine. Say them together at bedtime or write them on little notes for their lunchbox. This way, your child will hear and believe these positive messages.

Another powerful way to build your child's self-esteem is by encouraging them to engage in activities they love. Whether painting, playing a musical instrument, or playing a sport, these activities let your child experience success and enjoyment outside school. Show genuine interest and pride in what they do. Cheer them on and celebrate their progress. This helps them develop a strong sense of identity that isn't dependent on their narcissistic parent's approval. They'll start to feel competent, which can help them deal with criticism.

Your behavior also plays a massive role in shaping your child's self-image. Show them what self-respect looks like. Set and respect your boundaries and engage in activities that make you happy. Talk about your hobbies and interests with your child. When they see you enjoying your passions, they learn that having and pursuing their interests is essential. This shows them that their life should be filled with joy and not just focused on meeting others' expectations.

Positive reinforcement is vital in building your child's self-esteem. Acknowledge and praise their efforts, not just their achievements. Celebrate their big and small successes. This shifts the focus from outcomes, which they can't always control, to their efforts, which they can. Whether they score a soccer goal or help with chores at home, let them know you appreciate their hard work. This allows them to understand that their efforts matter and makes them feel valued.

By using affirmations, encouraging their interests, modeling positive behavior, and reinforcing their efforts, you create an environment that fosters a positive self-image in your child. This environment helps buffer against the negative impacts of a narcissistic parent's behavior. Your child will grow up with a stable sense of self-worth and the emotional resilience to face life's challenges confidently.

In doing so, you not only counteract potential damage from the narcissistic influence but also empower your child to build their own identity rooted in positivity and self-respect. Your efforts make a huge difference in helping your child feel good about themselves and their place in the world.

Make a Difference with Your Review

Unlock the Power of Generosity

"Strength doesn't come from what you can do. It comes from overcoming the things you once thought you couldn't." - Rikki Rogers

Hey there! Let's take a moment to talk about something super important that doesn't cost a dime but can make a huge difference. I'm talking about giving a little gift to someone you don't know just because you can.

We all know how challenging co-parenting can be, especially when you're dealing with a narcissist. It's tough; sometimes, it feels like you're walking on a tightrope with no safety net. But here's the thing: sharing your experience and insights from this book can be a safety net for someone struggling. Imagine being in their shoes, looking for guidance, and not knowing where to turn. Your review could be the helping hand they need.

Our mission with this book is simple: to make co-parenting with a narcissist less of a nightmare and more of a manageable reality. We want to reach everyone who can use guidance, empathy, and hope for a brighter future.

And here's where you come in. Yep, you! Your review can be a beacon of hope for someone searching for answers. Think of it as a small, kind gesture that could change a struggling parent's life. Whether they're trying to maintain their sanity, protect their kids, or just figure out how to communicate without tearing their hair out, your words could make all the difference.

So, here's my big ask: would you leave a review for this book? It doesn't have to be fancy or long—just a few honest words about how it helped you. It won't cost you anything but a few seconds of your time and could mean the world to someone else.

To share your thoughts, simply scan the QR code below or visit this link:

[https://www.amazon.com/review/review-your-purchases/?asin= BOOKASIN]

[QR]

If you like to pay it forward, you're my kind of person. Welcome to the club! Together, we can make co-parenting more manageable and less lonely.

Thank you from the bottom of my heart for participating in this journey. Now, let's dive back into our adventure together.

Your biggest fan, Jenna Lexington

Jenna Lexington

PS - Here's a fun thought: sharing something valuable with others makes you invaluable. If this book could help a fellow co-parent, please pass it along. Spread the love and the knowledge!

Make a Difference with Your Review

Unlock the Power of Generosity

"Strength doesn't come from what you can do. It comes from overcoming the things you once thought you couldn't." - Rikki Rogers

Hey there! Let's take a moment to talk about something super important that doesn't cost a dime but can make a huge difference. I'm talking about giving a little gift to someone you don't know just because you can.

We all know how challenging co-parenting can be, especially when you're dealing with a narcissist. It's tough; sometimes, it feels like walking on a tightrope with no safety net. But here's the thing: sharing your experience and insights from this book can be a safety net for someone struggling. Imagine being in their shoes, looking for guidance, and not knowing where to turn. Your review could be the helping hand they need.

Our mission with this book is simple: to make co-parenting with a narcissist less of a nightmare and more of a manageable reality. We want to reach everyone who can use guidance, empathy, and hope for a brighter future.

And here's where you come in. Yep, you! Your review can be a beacon of hope for someone searching for answers. Think of it as a small, kind gesture that could change a struggling parent's life. Whether they're trying to maintain their sanity, protect their kids, or figure out how to communicate without tearing their hair out, your words could make all the difference.

So, here's my big ask: would you leave a review for this book? It doesn't have to be fancy or long—just a few honest words about how it helped you. It won't cost you anything but a few seconds of your time and could mean the world to someone else.

To share your thoughts, scan the QR code below or visit this link: https://www.amazon.com/review/review-your-purchases/?asin= B0DF31FPC2

If you like to pay it forward, you're my kind of person. Welcome to the club! Together, we can make co-parenting more manageable and less lonely.

Thank you from the bottom of my heart for participating in this journey. Now, let's dive back into our adventure together.

Your biggest fan, Jenna Lexington

Jenna Lexington

PS - Here's a fun thought: sharing something valuable with others makes you invaluable. If this book could help a fellow co-parent, please pass it along. Spread the love and the knowledge!

SIX

Handling Finances

D ivorce can be challenging, especially when it messes up your finances. After years of high legal fees and moving to a single-income household, you might feel like starting from scratch. Some people even face bankruptcy. It's okay to feel overwhelmed but remember, you can get through this. Let's take it step by step.

6.1 Assessing Your Financial Situation

First, let's figure out where you stand financially. Start by listing all your current income sources and amounts. This includes your job, child support, alimony, and any other money coming in. Next, write down all your expenses. Include fixed costs like rent and utilities and variable expenses like groceries and transportation.

A basic budget can help you see where your money goes each month. Remember to include your debts, such as credit card balances, loans, and bankruptcy proceedings. Knowing your financial situation is the first step to taking control.

6.2 Setting Up a Basic Budget

Alright, let's dive into setting up a budget! This might sound boring, but trust me, it's beneficial. It's like a plan for your money so you can see where it's going and how you can save more of it. Here's how you can do it step by step:

First things first, write down your essential expenses. These are the things you need to live:

- **Housing**: Rent or mortgage payments.
- **Utilities**: Electricity, water, gas, and internet.
- **Food**: Groceries and eating out.
- **Transportation**: Gas, bus fare, or any other travel costs.

You must pay these bills, the ones you can't skip. Knowing how much you spend on them monthly gives you a clear picture of your necessary expenses.

Now, let's look at where else your money is going. Write down everything you spend money on for one month—from that morning coffee to a new pair of shoes. This will help you see exactly where your money goes and where you might be able to cut back.

You can track your spending in different ways:

- **Apps**: Many free apps make it easy to track spending. Some good ones are Mint, YNAB (You Need A Budget), and PocketGuard.
- **Spreadsheets**: If you like using your computer, you can record your expenses using a simple spreadsheet. Programs like Excel or Google Sheets work great for this.
- **Notebook**: If you prefer old-school methods, a notebook works just fine. Just jot down your expenses each day.

After you've tracked your spending for a month, review it. Are there areas where you can cut back? Maybe you're spending more on eating out than you realized, or those subscription services are adding up.

Here are some common areas where people can often save money:

- **Eating Out**: Try cooking at home more often. It's usually cheaper and healthier.
- **Entertainment**: Look for free or low-cost activities. Libraries often have free events, or you can enjoy parks and community activities.
- **Subscriptions**: Do you need all those streaming services? Cut back to just one or two.
- **Shopping**: Ask yourself if you need that new item or if it's just an impulse buy.

Your budget isn't something you set once and forget. It's a tool you adjust as needed. Each month, look at your budget and see how you did. Did you stick to it? Did you overspend in some areas? Use this information to adjust your spending and savings goals for the next month.

Setting up a budget is a significant first step, but the key is to stick with it. Make it a habit to review your budget regularly. This might be once a week, once every two weeks, or at least once a month. The more you check in with your budget, the easier it becomes to stick to it and make intelligent financial choices.

Remember to celebrate your successes! Did you manage to cut back on eating out? Great job! Did you make all your debt payments this month? Fantastic! Each step you take towards managing your money better is a win. Celebrate these small victories to keep yourself motivated.

Setting up a budget might seem daunting initially, but it's a powerful tool for managing your finances. With a clear plan, you'll feel more confident about where your money goes and how to make the most of it. Keep at it, and remember, every little bit helps! You've got this!

6.3 Managing Debt and Bankruptcy

If you're facing bankruptcy, it can feel overwhelming but don't panic. You can take steps to manage it and start rebuilding your financial stability.

First, let's understand what bankruptcy is. Bankruptcy is a legal process that can help you get relief from your debts if you can't pay them. It might sound scary, but it's a tool designed to help you get a fresh start. There are different types of bankruptcy, but the most common for individuals are Chapter 7 and Chapter 13.

- **Chapter 7**: This is also known as "liquidation bankruptcy." It involves selling some of your assets to pay off your debts. The process is relatively quick, usually lasting a few months.
- **Chapter 13**: This is called "reorganization bankruptcy." It allows you to keep your assets but requires you to follow a court-approved repayment plan over three to five years.

Steps to Take

1. **Negotiate with Creditors**

Before you file for bankruptcy, try negotiating with your creditors. Explain your situation honestly. Many creditors would rather get something rather than nothing, so they might be willing to lower your payments or interest rates. For example, you could say, "I'm struggling to make ends meet right now. Can we work out a payment plan that I can afford?"

1. **Create a Repayment Plan**

If you're filing for Chapter 13 bankruptcy, you must create a repayment plan outlining how to repay your debts over the next few years. The court must approve this plan. It can be helpful to work with a bankruptcy attorney to ensure that your plan is realistic and fair.

1. **Make Minimum Payments**

Whether you're in bankruptcy or not, making at least the minimum payments on your debts is essential. This helps you avoid extra fees and penalties, which can make your debt grow even more. Set up reminders or automatic payments to ensure you don't miss any payments.

1. **Seek Debt Counseling**

If you're feeling lost, seek help from debt counseling services. These organizations offer free or low-cost advice on managing your debts. They can help you create a budget, negotiate with creditors, and set up a repayment plan. Look for nonprofit organizations that often provide the best support without trying to sell you something.

1. **Prioritize Debts**

Not all debts are the same. Some debts, like your mortgage or car loan, might be more important to pay off first because you don't want to lose your home or car. Other debts, like credit cards, might have higher interest rates, so paying those off first can save you money in the long run. Prioritize your debts based on your situation.

1. **Stay Positive and Patient**

Getting out of debt and managing bankruptcy takes time. It's a slow process, but every step you take gets you closer to financial stability. Celebrate your small victories along the way. Have you paid off a credit card? That's a big win! Have you saved up $100 in your emergency fund? Fantastic!

Remember, bankruptcy isn't the end of the world. It's a tool to help you get a fresh start. By negotiating with creditors, making at least minimum payments, seeking debt counseling, prioritizing your debts, cutting unnecessary spending, building an emergency fund, staying positive and patient, educating yourself, and getting professional help, you can manage your debt and work towards a more stable financial future. You've got this! Keep going, and don't hesitate to ask for help when needed.

6.4 Finding Additional Income

Extra income sometimes makes a big difference, especially when working with a tight budget. Let's look at some practical ways to earn more money.

One way to boost your income is to take on a side job or freelance work. There are many options, and you can choose something that fits your skills and schedule.

- **Online Freelancing**: Websites like Upwork, Fiverr, and Freelancer allow you to offer services like writing, graphic design, or data entry. You can work from home and choose projects that fit your availability.
- **Part-Time Jobs**: Look for part-time jobs in your area. Retail, food service, and customer service positions often have flexible hours that can work around your main job and family responsibilities.
- **Gig Economy**: Platforms like Uber, Lyft, DoorDash, and Instacart offer opportunities to earn extra money by driving or delivering food and groceries. These gigs often let you set your hours, making it easier to fit into your schedule.

Investing in your skills and education can lead to better job opportunities and higher income.

- **Job Training Programs**: Look for local job training programs to help you learn new skills. Community colleges and workforce development centers often offer healthcare, IT, and trade courses.

- **Online Courses**: Websites like Coursera, Udemy, and Khan Academy offer accessible or affordable courses on various subjects. You can learn quickly and gain valuable skills to improve your job prospects.
- **Certifications**: Some professions offer certifications that can make you more competitive in the job market. For example, getting certified in project management, digital marketing, or coding can open up new career opportunities.

Selling items you no longer need can be a quick way to make extra cash.

- **Online Marketplaces**: Platforms like eBay, Facebook Marketplace, and Craigslist make it easy to sell items like clothes, electronics, and furniture. To attract buyers, attract buyers, take clear photos, write honest descriptions, and price your y.
- **Garage Sales**: If you have many items to sell, consider hosting a garage sale. Advertise it in your neighborhood and online to draw in more people. This can be a great way to declutter your home and make some money at the same time.
- **Consignment Shops**: Some local stores will sell your items for you and give you a percentage of the sale. This can be a good option for selling higher-end clothing, accessories, or furniture.

Sometimes, thinking outside the box can lead to unexpected income opportunities.

- **Rent Out Space**: If you have extra space in your home, consider renting it out. Websites like Airbnb allow you to rent a room or your entire house to travelers. Just check local regulations and ensure they are allowed in your area.

- **Pet Sitting or Dog Walking**: If you love animals, consider offering pet sitting or dog walking services. Apps like Rover and Wag make connecting with pet owners who need help easy.
- **Tutoring**: If you excel in a particular subject, offer tutoring services. You can tutor students in your community or offer services online through Tutor.com or Chegg Tutors.

While finding additional income can provide immediate relief, it's also essential to consider the long term.

- **Career Advancement**: Look for opportunities to advance in your current job. Talk to your boss about your career goals and ask for advice. Sometimes, taking on additional responsibilities can lead to promotions and pay raises.
- **Networking**: Connect with professionals in your field to learn about new job opportunities. Attend local networking events, join professional organizations, and use LinkedIn to build your professional network.

Extra income can significantly improve your financial situation, especially during tough times. You can boost your income and work towards more excellent financial stability by exploring side jobs, investing in your skills, selling unused items, and thinking creatively. Keep an open mind, be proactive, and remember that every little bit helps. You've got this!

6.5 Cutting Costs

Finding ways to cut costs can make a big difference in your budget, freeing up money for other needs or saving for the future. Here are some practical tips to help you reduce your everyday expenses.

Coupons and discounts can save you a lot of money on everyday purchases.

- **Grocery Coupons**: Look for coupons in your local newspaper, online coupon websites, and store apps. Many grocery stores have loyalty programs that offer additional discounts and digital coupons.
- **Discount Apps**: Use apps like Honey, Rakuten, and RetailMeNot to find discounts and cashback offers on online purchases. These apps can help you save money without much effort.
- **Store Sales**: Look for sales and stock up on non-perishable items when discounted. Seasonal sales, clearance events, and holiday promotions can offer significant savings.

Meal planning can help you avoid unnecessary food spending and reduce waste.

- **Weekly Meal Plan**: Create a weekly meal plan and shopping list. Stick to your list when you shop to avoid impulse buys.
- **Cook in Bulk**: Prepare large batches of meals and freeze leftovers for future use. This saves time and money and ensures home-cooked meals are ready when needed.
- **Use Leftovers**: Use leftovers to create new meals. For example, use leftover chicken in salads, sandwiches, or soups.

Entertainment doesn't have to be expensive. There are plenty of fun activities that cost little to nothing.

- **Libraries**: Libraries offer free access to books, movies, and music. Many also host free events and activities for all ages, such as storytimes, workshops, and book clubs.
- **Parks and Recreation**: Explore local parks for hiking, picnicking, and free community events. Check out community centers for free or low-cost classes and activities.

- **Streaming Services**: If you have multiple streaming subscriptions, consider cutting back to just one or two. Look for free streaming options or use free trials to watch your favorite shows and movies.

Subscriptions and memberships can add up quickly. Review them regularly to ensure you only pay for what you use.

- **Gym Memberships**: If you're not using your gym membership, consider canceling it and looking for free workout options like running, home workouts, or community fitness classes.
- **Magazine and Newspaper Subscriptions**: If you have magazine or newspaper subscriptions you don't read, cancel them. Many publications offer free online content.
- **Streaming Services**: As mentioned earlier, limit the number of streaming services you subscribe to—share subscriptions with family or friends to save money.

Lowering your utility bills can lead to significant savings.

- **Energy Efficiency**: Use energy-efficient light bulbs, unplug electronics when not in use, and adjust your thermostat to save on heating and cooling costs.
- **Water Conservation**: Fix leaks, take shorter showers, and use water-saving appliances to reduce your water bill.
- **Bundling Services**: If you have separate providers for internet, cable, and phone services, consider bundling them with one provider for a discount.

Being a savvy shopper can help you get more value for your money.

- **Buy Generic Brands**: Generic or store-brand products are often just as good as name brands and cost less.
- **Thrift Stores**: Shop at thrift stores for clothing, furniture,

and household items. You can find great deals on gently used items.

- **Price Comparison**: Compare prices before making significant purchases. Use price comparison websites or apps to find the best deals.

Transportation costs can be a big part of your budget. Here are some ways to cut those costs.

- **Carpooling**: Share rides with coworkers, friends, or family members to save on gas and reduce wear and tear on your vehicle.
- **Public Transportation**: Use public transportation when possible. It's often cheaper than driving, and you can save on parking fees and vehicle maintenance.
- **Biking and Walking**: Consider biking instead of driving for short trips. It's good for your health and your wallet.

Doing things yourself can save money on services and repairs.

- **Home Repairs**: Learn to handle simple home repairs yourself. Many online tutorials can guide you through basic tasks.
- **Personal Care**: Consider doing home manicures, haircuts, or other tasks. There are plenty of online resources to help you learn how.

These tips can reduce your everyday expenses and save money for other priorities. Remember, every little bit helps; small changes can add significant savings over time. You've got this! Keep looking for ways to save, and your financial situation will improve.

6.6 When Ex Refuses to Pay

Dealing with an ex who refuses to follow a court order and won't pay their share of expenses can be frustrating and stressful. Here are steps you can take to address this situation:

First, review the court order closely. Ensure you understand what your ex should pay for and when those payments are due. This will help you understand your rights and prepare you to take further steps.

Keep detailed records of all the expenses that your ex is supposed to share. Save receipts, invoices, and any other proof of payment. Also, record all the times you have asked your ex to pay their share, including dates and how you communicated with them (email, text, etc.). This documentation will be crucial if you need to take legal action.

Try to communicate with your ex about the missed payments. Be clear and polite. Sometimes, a simple reminder can resolve the issue. For example, you can send an email or text message saying:

"Hi [Ex], I wanted to remind you about the court-ordered expenses for [Child]. According to the court order, you owe $[amount] for [specific expense]. Please let me know when you can make this payment. Thank you."

If direct communication doesn't work, consider seeking mediation. This can be less stressful and less expensive than going to court. If mediation doesn't work, it might be time to contact your attorney. They can provide legal advice on the best way to proceed. Your attorney can help you understand your rights and the legal options to enforce the court order.

One legal option is to file a motion for contempt of court. This means you are asking the court to enforce the order because your ex is not complying. If the court finds your ex in contempt, they may be ordered to pay the outstanding expenses, and in some cases, they may face fines or other penalties.

You can contact your local child support enforcement agency if child support payments are involved. They can enforce child support orders by garnishing wages, seizing tax refunds, and suspending driver's licenses to ensure payments.

It can be discouraging when your ex refuses to follow the court order but stay positive and persistent. Keep documenting everything and follow the legal steps necessary to enforce the order. Remember, you're doing this to meet your children's needs.

SEVEN

Co-parenting vs. Parallel Parenting

I magine trying to work with someone who always wants their way. That's what it can feel like trying to co-parent with a narcissistic ex. This chapter helps you determine whether co-parenting is possible and how to do it in a way that keeps your kids' well-being front and center.

7.1 Is Co-parenting Possible?

Co-parenting with a narcissist depends a lot on their behavior. Sometimes, if the narcissist can follow structured rules and recognize their actions, co-parenting might work. For example, if they can stick to agreements about visitations or decision-making, you might find some cooperation. But remember, even in the best situations, you're likely to face emotional manipulation and conflicts.

Take Emily's situation. She managed a fragile co-parenting setup with her narcissistic ex by only communicating through a digital co-parenting platform. This platform helped them schedule visits and appointments without direct conversations, reducing chances for conflict. This worked because it limited opportunities for her ex to manipulate or escalate disputes.

When you co-parent with a narcissist, set realistic expectations. Know that challenges will pop up often, and emotional manipulations will be part of it. Expect that you might have to make more compromises to keep the peace. Understand that traditional co-parenting, which relies on mutual respect and open communication, might not fully apply to your situation.

In Emily's case, regular sessions with a family therapist helped her and her ex handle co-parenting challenges. The therapist provided a controlled environment that balanced the power dynamics and gave Emily tools to interact with her ex more effectively, always focusing on their children's well-being.

Navigating co-parenting with a narcissist means understanding the challenges, preparing for them, and using the right tools and support. By assessing what's possible, setting clear boundaries, managing interactions strategically, and involving professionals, you can create a co-parenting setup that prioritizes and protects your children's well-being above all else.

7.2 The Basics of Parallel Parenting

Sometimes, co-parenting just doesn't work out, especially when there's a lot of conflict with your ex. That's where parallel parenting comes in. This method lets you and your ex handle parenting duties separately, reducing the need for direct communication and minimizing conflict.

In parallel parenting, each parent takes care of their responsibilities without talking much to the other parent. Instead of having extended discussions, you share only the necessary information about your kids. For example, you might use an online calendar to update your ex about doctor's appointments or school events. This way, you avoid arguments and keep things calm for everyone.

To make parallel parenting work, you need a clear and detailed plan. Write and legally document this plan, so parents know their roles and responsibilities. It will include details like who makes certain decisions, the holiday schedule, and what to do in emergencies. Communication should be structured and limited to what's necessary. Parenting apps help with this by recording all exchanges and ensuring documentation of everything.

The benefits of parallel parenting in high-conflict situations are significant. By reducing the amount of interaction with your ex, you minimize the stress and instability that constant arguments can create. For your children, this approach provides a stable and predictable environment. They won't have to witness as many arguments or feel caught in the middle of disputes. Plus, it allows you to focus on your relationship with your kids without interference from your ex.

Setting and maintaining strict boundaries is vital in parallel parenting. You might need legal help to make sure these boundaries are respected. For example, you can set specific times or days for phone calls and restrict in-person interactions during exchanges. Transitions can happen at school or in a neutral location to avoid personal contact. It might be tough to enforce these boundaries if your ex tests the limits, but staying consistent and having legal backing can help keep things in check.

Using these strategies, you protect your emotional and mental health and shield your children from ongoing conflict. Parallel parenting doesn't fix the issues with your ex, but it does offer a way to move forward. By focusing on what you can control—your actions and responses—you create a stable, peaceful environment where your children can thrive. Stay strong, and remember, you're doing the right thing for your family.

7.3 Transitioning from Co-parenting to Parallel Parenting

Sometimes, co-parenting just doesn't work out, especially when it causes too many arguments and stress for your kids. When that happens, it might be time to switch to parallel parenting. This isn't just a change in how you handle things but a significant shift in how you manage parenting with your ex.

The current co-parenting setup doesn't work because simple decisions lead to big fights and stress your kids out. Decisions like picking extracurricular activities or holiday plans lead to drawn-out disagreements. If your children seem anxious and stressed, or their behavior changes because of these disputes, it's a sign that co-parenting isn't sustainable.

Switching to parallel parenting involves several steps. Start by looking at what's causing the most conflict in your current setup. Think about how parallel parenting could help reduce these problems. You'll need to revisit custody agreements to adjust them for parallel parenting. This might mean creating detailed schedules or reducing the need for direct communication between you and your ex. A legal professional who knows about high-conflict parenting can help you draft a new parenting plan that minimizes interaction but ensures both parents meet their responsibilities.

When you talk to your kids about these changes, do it with care and sensitivity. Reassure them that both parents still love and support them, but some things will change to reduce stress and make life better for everyone. Explain the new setup in simple terms they can understand. For younger kids, say that Mommy and Daddy will have separate times with them but will both be at important events. For older kids, you can explain more and discuss how less direct contact between parents reduces conflict.

The adjustment period can be challenging for both you and your kids. Keeping routines and schedules consistent provides stability and security. Pay attention to how your kids respond and give extra support if they struggle with the transition. Spend more one-on-one time with them, do activities they enjoy, or seek help from a child psychologist who can offer strategies to help them cope with the changes. For yourself, adjust how you communicate with your ex and stick to the new boundaries set in your parallel parenting plan. Stay committed to these new routines because consistency will help everyone adapt.

By carefully managing each step, from recognizing the need for change to supporting your kids through the transition, you can move from co-parenting to parallel parenting in a way that focuses on your children's emotional health and well-being. This new approach requires careful planning and ongoing effort but can lead to a more peaceful and structured parenting arrangement. This shift will shield your kids from constant conflict and allow you to focus on nurturing and supporting them through this new phase of life.

7.4 Maintaining Communication in Parallel Parenting

When communicating with your ex, focus on the kids' needs and well-being. This isn't the time to bring up old arguments or unresolved issues from your relationship. For example, if your child has a new doctor, just share the doctor's name, contact information, and the first appointment date. Don't add personal comments about past disagreements. Keeping the communication strictly about the kids helps keep things professional and reduces the chance of conflict.

Setting clear rules about how and when to communicate is also important. Decide together how often you will update each other and through which methods. You might agree to use emails for general updates and texts only for urgent matters. Setting specific times for communication can also help. For example, you might decide that only emergency messages should be sent via text. This prevents one parent from feeling overwhelmed by constant messages and avoids late-night texts that can cause anxiety and sleepless nights.

Even with the best plans, miscommunications can happen. When they do, having a strategy to manage them is critical. Always start by seeking clarification. If you get an unclear email from your ex, politely ask for more details. This can help clear up misunderstandings before they turn into more significant issues. If miscommunications happen or your ex repeatedly breaks the communication rules, you should involve a mediator or seek legal advice. For example, suppose your ex ignores the agreed-upon communication methods, causing confusion or conflict. In that case, mediation can help reinforce these boundaries and keep the focus on your kids' best interests.

Navigating communication in parallel parenting doesn't mean you have to walk on eggshells, but it does require clear guidelines and a commitment to follow them. By using structured communication methods, focusing strictly on the kids' needs, setting clear rules, and handling miscommunications carefully, you can create a system that supports effective parenting while reducing the emotional strain on everyone. This approach allows you to enjoy the joys of parenting without getting bogged down by the challenges of interacting with a difficult ex, creating a healthier environment for your kids to grow and thrive.

7.5 Managing Special Occasions and Transitions

Special occasions and transitions between homes can be emotional and tricky, especially in a parallel parenting setup. Holidays, birthdays, and other significant events can be challenging, but with some careful planning, you can make these times happy and stress-free for your kids.

First, make plans well in advance. Set clear expectations ahead of time for events like school performances or graduations, which both parents might want to attend. Talk with your ex about the importance of keeping things peaceful and focusing on your child's experience. If celebrating separately works better, plan your own particular time. For example, if your ex has the kids on Christmas Day, you could have a festive Christmas Eve dinner instead.

Transitions between homes need preparation and consistency. Kids do best with a routine, so keep the exchange schedule regular. Talk to your kids about the plan, pack together, and make sure they know when and where the exchange will happen. This can help ease any anxiety they might feel. To avoid direct interaction with your ex, consider using a neutral location like a school or community center. This reduces the chance of conflict and keeps the focus on the kids.

Flexibility is essential, especially for special occasions and transitions. While routines are imperative, life can be unpredictable. Being flexible shows your child that their interests and commitments matter. If a significant event falls outside the regular schedule, being willing to adjust can make a big difference. Just make sure to communicate clearly and document any changes to prevent misunderstandings.

Creating new traditions can help your kids feel secure and valued. These new traditions can replace old ones and create positive memories. For example, if you used to have a big family gathering on Thanksgiving, you might start a new tradition of a Thanksgiving morning breakfast or a special weekend outing. Despite changes, these traditions show your kids they still have meaningful and joyful experiences.

Handling special occasions and transitions in a parallel parenting setup doesn't have to be stressful. Careful planning, clear communication, flexibility, and new traditions can make these times happy and peaceful. This approach helps your kids feel loved and secure, no matter what. These strategies make parallel parenting smoother and support children's well-being and happiness.

EIGHT

Addressing Specific Challenges

Co-parenting with a narcissistic ex can be especially tough when you're dealing with situations that go beyond everyday challenges. This could include things like your ex remarrying, moving far away or even to another country, or facing smear campaigns. This section will share practical advice and strategies for handling these tricky situations. Understanding these unique circumstances can help you be better prepared and create a healthier, more stable environment for you and your children.

8.1 When Your Ex Remarries

When your ex gets married again, your co-parenting situation can change. A new spouse might bring a different vibe to how your ex approaches parenting. They could have new ideas about discipline, bedtime routines, or even the kind of snacks the kids eat. You might start noticing changes in how your ex spends time with the kids, how involved they are in school activities, or even how they communicate with you. Taking a step back and observing these changes without jumping to conclusions is essential. Pay attention to how your ex's behavior shifts, how they interact with the kids, and any differences in their communication with you. This will give you a clearer picture of any adjustments you need.

With a new spouse in the mix, how you communicate with your ex might need to change. Setting clear boundaries and defining everyone's roles early on can save a lot of headaches down the road. Writing down what's acceptable and not regarding communication can be helpful. For instance, decide what kind of information your ex should share with you directly and what can be handled by the new spouse. This clarity can prevent misunderstandings and keep interactions respectful and focused on the kids. Choosing a communication method that works for everyone, like emails, texts, or even a co-parenting app, can help keep things straightforward and on track.

The new family dynamics might also mean it's time to examine custody arrangements again. If your ex's remarriage changes your kids' daily routines or living situation, revisiting the current custody agreement might be necessary. This isn't about fighting for custody without good reason; it's about ensuring the arrangement is still the best fit for your kids. For example, if the new marriage leads to a move or significant changes in the household, these could be valid reasons to review and possibly adjust the custody terms. Gather all the facts and document why these changes are in the kids' best interest.

Your ex getting remarried can also impact legal matters, like financial obligations. A new marriage could alter the financial landscape, affecting child support or other responsibilities. It's wise to consult a legal professional to understand how these changes might impact you and your children. They can guide you through any adjustments to support arrangements or custody agreements that might be necessary.

Navigating your ex's remarriage involves being patient, observant, and ready to make strategic changes. Understanding the new family dynamics, updating how you communicate, re-evaluating custody arrangements, and staying on top of the legal aspects will ensure that your co-parenting relationship adapts smoothly to the new situation. Keeping your kids' stability and well-being at the heart of these adjustments is critical to making this transition as smooth as possible.

Introducing a new spouse can also influence the emotional environment of your children. They may feel excited about gaining a new family member or experience anxiety about changes in their home life. It's important to acknowledge their feelings and provide a space for them to express their thoughts and concerns. You might notice them acting out or withdrawing as they process these changes. Encourage open communication, letting them know it's okay to feel confused or unsure about what's happening. Reassure them that your love and support remain constant, no matter how family structures change.

A new spouse might also bring their children into the mix, creating a blended family scenario. This can add another layer of complexity to the situation as your children adjust to new siblings and the dynamics that come with them. It's essential to monitor how these relationships develop and address any issues, whether sibling rivalry or feelings of exclusion. Encouraging positive interactions and setting clear expectations for behavior can help smooth the transition and foster a sense of unity and belonging.

As you navigate these changes, it's crucial to maintain a positive and open attitude. Avoid badmouthing the new spouse or your ex in front of the kids, as this can create additional stress and confusion for them. Instead, focus on reinforcing that despite things being different, both parents are committed to their well-being. This approach helps build a cooperative co-parenting environment where your children feel secure and supported by all the adults in their lives.

8.2 International and Long-Distance Co-Parenting

Co-parenting from a distance, especially across different countries, can be challenging. When you and your ex live far apart, it's not just about dealing with the usual co-parenting stuff; you must also figure out legal and logistical issues. Different countries and states have rules about custody and parental rights, which can make things tricky. For instance, some places require special permission to take kids out of the country or state, affecting travel plans and decisions about where your kids live. Understanding these laws is super important, so talking to a lawyer who knows international family law can be helpful. They can guide you through the legal maze and make sure you're doing everything by the book, which can prevent arguments with your ex.

Connecting across different time zones can be tricky, but technology can help. Co-parenting apps are great for managing and documenting your interactions so both parents stay in the loop about what's going on with the kids. Regular video calls are a must —they help you maintain a face-to-face connection with your kids so you don't miss out on their daily lives and memorable moments. For example, you can have virtual dinner dates, eat together over video chat, or read bedtime stories to them. These little rituals can make a big difference. Also, using emails or messaging to update each other about school, health, and other important stuff helps keep everyone informed. Setting up these communication routines early on is critical. For example, you might agree to have a video call every Sunday evening and check in via text several times during the week. This helps your kids feel connected to both parents, even if one is far away.

When it comes to travel for visitations, planning is crucial. This isn't just about buying plane tickets; it's about ensuring everything goes smoothly. Start by setting up an explicit visit schedule, including how often they happen and who will pay for what. For example, you might agree that one parent covers the cost of flights while the other handles transportation once the kids arrive. Discuss and agree on these details in advance, and put everything in writing. Safety is also a big concern, especially if the kids travel alone. For younger kids, consider using a service that provides a chaperone to accompany them. For older kids, set up rules for checking in during travel, like texting when they board a plane or arrive at their destination. Keeping a detailed record of all travel plans and communications can help avoid misunderstandings and ensure everyone is on the same page.

Providing emotional support to your kids is as important as handling the logistics. Being far away from one parent can be hard on kids, and they might feel confused or sad. It's important to talk to them openly about their feelings and reassure them that both parents love them, even from a distance. For example, after a visit, you might ask, "How did it go? What was your favorite part?" This shows them that you care and want to hear about their experiences. Maintaining routines like weekly video calls or sending care packages with little treats or notes can help kids feel connected and loved. Encourage them to express their thoughts and feelings, whether excited, sad, or anything in between. You can say, "It's okay to miss mom/dad, and it's okay to talk about it." Getting a child psychologist or counselor involved can be helpful. They can provide a safe space for your kids to talk about their feelings and offer strategies to cope with the challenges of long-distance co-parenting.

In this situation, being organized and proactive is vital. Knowing the legal aspects, using technology to stay connected, planning travel carefully, and providing emotional support can help you manage the complexities of international and long-distance co-parenting. Focusing on these areas allows you to maintain a strong relationship with your kids and ensure their well-being, even when you're miles apart.

8.3 Narcissistic Rage

Dealing with an ex's outbursts can be stressful, especially when they're prone to narcissistic rage. This type of anger often flares up quickly and intensely when they feel criticized or perceive an attack on their ego. It's helpful to recognize the early signs that things are about to get heated so you can manage the situation and protect your peace of mind.

You might notice your ex criticizing you more often, using sarcasm, or changing their tone to show annoyance or anger. Sometimes, the signs are more blatant, like slamming doors or glaring. Verbal attacks are another clear warning sign. When these behaviors appear, it's an excellent moment to shift your approach and try some de-escalation techniques. We've covered a few strategies in previous chapters, but if those don't work, here are a few more that might help.

Use of Reflective Listening

This involves calmly restating the other person's words without agreeing or disagreeing. It shows that you are listening but does not validate their negative emotions. For instance, if the narcissist says, "You never support me," you can respond with, "You feel like I'm not supportive." This technique helps de-escalate the situation by making them feel heard without engaging in their accusations.

Setting Time Limits

When you anticipate a potentially heated conversation, set a precise time limit for the discussion. This can prevent the situation from dragging on and escalating further. You might say, "I can discuss this for the next 15 minutes, but then I need to focus on other responsibilities." This approach keeps interactions brief and controlled, reducing the chance of a prolonged conflict.

Practicing Self-Distancing

This technique involves mentally distancing yourself from the situation to avoid getting emotionally caught up. You can do this by imagining the situation as if you're an outsider observing it or thinking about how you would advise a friend in the same situation. This perspective helps you stay calm and detached, making it easier to respond rationally rather than emotionally.

Strategic Validation

Sometimes, offering a small, non-committal form of validation can help calm the narcissist without feeding their ego excessively. This might involve acknowledging their feelings without agreeing with their viewpoint. For example, you could say, "I see that this is important to you," without conceding to their demands. This can reduce tension and allow for a more productive conversation.

Establishing "Exit Strategies"

Plan for how you'll leave the situation if it gets too heated. This could involve having a prearranged signal with a friend to call you or planning an excuse to leave. For instance, you might say, "I have to go now, but we can discuss this later when we've both had time to think." Knowing you have a way out can reduce anxiety and help you stay calm.

Mindfulness and Grounding Techniques

During an episode of narcissistic rage, practice mindfulness by focusing on your breath or grounding yourself through physical sensations. This can help you stay present and centered, preventing you from reacting impulsively. For example, you can focus on the sensation of your feet on the ground or the feeling of a small object in your hand.

Disengaging from Gaslighting

Narcissists may use gaslighting to make you doubt your reality. Recognize when this happens and reaffirm your perceptions. You can use phrases like, "I remember things differently" or "I know what I experienced." This technique helps maintain your sense of reality and prevents you from getting drawn into their manipulations.

If, despite your best efforts, the situation continues to escalate, sometimes the best thing to do is to end the interaction. This could mean politely excusing yourself from a phone call or finding a way to leave the situation if you're in person. Your safety and mental well-being are the top priorities, so don't hesitate to step away if things get out of hand.

When narcissistic rage turns into something more threatening, it's essential to consider your legal and safety options. If you ever feel unsafe, don't hesitate to involve the authorities to protect yourself and your kids. Documenting any incidents of rage or threatening behavior is also a good idea. Keep detailed notes with dates, times, descriptions of what happened, and any witnesses. This documentation can be vital if you need legal action, like getting a restraining order or adjusting custody arrangements. A clear record can support your case and show that you're not making things up or overreacting.

Maintaining your emotional safety is just as important as physical safety. Affirmations can be an excellent tool for keeping your self-esteem intact. Remind yourself with phrases like, "I deserve to be treated with respect" or "I am strong and capable." These reminders can help you stay grounded and confident. It can also be helpful to have an emotional safety plan. This might include having a trusted friend you can call when things get rough, identifying a safe space where you can go to cool off, or engaging in activities that help you relax and regroup after a stressful encounter.

By using these strategies, you can better manage the challenges of narcissistic rage and maintain a sense of stability and security in your life. These techniques help you handle conflicts calmly and confidently, making even the most complex interactions easier to navigate. Remember, your well-being comes first; taking the necessary steps to protect it is okay.

8.4 Smear Campaigns and Public Defamation

When co-parenting becomes challenging, it can spill over into your public and professional life. Your co-parent might try to damage your reputation through smear campaigns and public defamation, aiming to hurt your standing and isolate you socially and professionally. Recognizing these tactics early can help you respond in a way that protects your integrity and reputation.

Smear campaigns often start subtly. It might begin with vague comments or insinuations that initially don't seem too bad. But over time, these can escalate into outright accusations and lies, spread in social circles or even on social media. For example, you might notice acquaintances acting differently toward you or colleagues hearing false information about you. You could even face direct attacks on social media, where the goal is to paint you as unstable or unreliable. These actions usually aim to provoke a reaction from you, which the other person can use to support their narrative. It's important to recognize these tactics early so that you can respond thoughtfully rather than emotionally, which helps minimize their impact.

When you face defamation, the legal system offers ways to protect your reputation and hold the responsible party accountable. One option is to send a cease and desist letter, formally requesting that the harmful behavior stop immediately. If the defamation continues, consider pursuing a restraining order or a defamation lawsuit. A restraining order can be appropriate if there's a direct threat to your safety or peace. At the same time, a defamation lawsuit focuses on recovering damages for the harm done to your reputation. It's crucial to document all instances of defamation carefully—save social media posts, record damaging statements made in public, and gather testimonials from witnesses. This documentation can serve as essential evidence if you decide to take legal action. Consulting with a lawyer specializing in defamation can help you explore your options and determine the best course of action for your situation.

Maintaining your professional and social reputation during a smear campaign requires a calm and strategic approach. Address false accusations directly with those affected to clear up misunderstandings and present your side of the story. Stick to the facts and communicate professionally, providing evidence to debunk false claims if necessary. Keep your responses focused on your qualifications and performance in your professional environment. A positive social media presence can also help counteract negative portrayals, highlighting your competence, integrity, and commitment in your personal and professional life.

Having a solid support system is crucial when dealing with the emotional toll of defamation. Family, friends, and professional networks can offer emotional support, practical advice, and affirmations of your character. Consider seeking professional counseling if the situation becomes particularly stressful or emotionally draining. A counselor or therapist experienced in dealing with complex relationships can provide strategies for managing stress, maintaining self-esteem, and navigating the emotions triggered by public character attacks. They can also guide you in communicating about the situation in your social and professional circles, helping you uphold your dignity and focus on moving forward positively.

NINE

Dealing with the Wider Family and Community

I magine walking into a room filled with family, friends, and familiar faces you know so well. Some people have smiles, while others might be wearing curious or concerned expressions. Emotions and expectations fill the air; you can sense the tension beneath the surface. Family gatherings, especially when a difficult ex is involved, can feel like navigating a delicate situation where you must carefully consider every word and action. You want to avoid awkward moments or unnecessary conflicts while ensuring your kids have a positive experience. This chapter is all about helping you manage these social situations gracefully. It's about finding ways to enjoy these events with your children, making happy memories, and not getting caught up in drama. We'll explore strategies and tips to make these gatherings smoother, allowing you and your kids more fun and less stress.

9.1 Family Gatherings

Family gatherings can bring up lots of memories and emotions. You must plan mentally and logistically. Start by setting realistic expectations—know that interactions might not always be smooth.

Prepare yourself for potential triggers that could upset the balance. Mentally rehearse how you'll handle possible confrontations to give yourself a sense of control and calmness. Logistically, plan the details of the gathering. Know the schedule, activities planned, and how they fit with your co-parenting arrangements.

Create a support plan. This might mean having a trusted family member or friend who understands your situation and can offer emotional support or step in if things get tough. Also, prepare a private space where you can take a moment to breathe and regroup. These preparations create a safety net, ensuring that you and your children can navigate the event with less tension and more enjoyment.

Plan for how you'll handle interactions at family gatherings. This can help set expectations and reduce conflict. Think about which topics of conversation you want to focus on and which sensitive subjects to avoid. If you need to step away from a situation, set up a discreet signal with your children or a support person so they know when to help.

Polite disengagement is a helpful skill to develop. When a conversation starts to go south or gets too personal, find a way to excuse yourself without causing a scene. You could say, "I need to check on the kids," or "I'd like to get some fresh air." These strategies help you avoid potential conflicts and set a good example for your children to handle uncomfortable situations.

Kids often pick up on the tension between parents, and family gatherings can intensify these feelings. To help them emotionally, talk to them beforehand about what to expect and reassure them that they're safe and you're there for them. Watch for signs that they might be feeling overwhelmed and step in before things get too intense.

Having private check-ins can be helpful. Find a quiet moment to ask your child how they're doing and let them know it's okay to feel upset or uncomfortable. These moments of support not only help them feel cared for but also give you a better understanding of how they're handling the situation. This way, they know they're not alone in dealing with their emotions and that their feelings matter.

9.2 Mutual Friends and Social Circles

Navigating shared social circles after a divorce can be a balancing act, especially when mutual friends are involved. Imagine getting an invitation to a birthday party or a holiday gathering and knowing your ex will be there, too. It can take time to decide whether to go or not. On the one hand, you want to maintain these friendships and be part of your social scene. On the other hand, you have to think about your emotional well-being and that of your kids. For example, if you're invited to a close friend's BBQ and know your ex will be there, think about the atmosphere. Will it be a relaxed, friendly environment where you can comfortably coexist? Or could it become a tense situation that leaves you stressed out? Sometimes, it's better to politely decline and suggest catching up with friends another time, allowing you to avoid unnecessary drama and keep your social life separate.

When talking with mutual friends about co-parenting issues, it's essential to be careful and thoughtful. You want their support but don't want to put them in a position where they feel they must choose sides. Let's say you're frustrated because your ex keeps canceling plans with the kids last minute. Instead of venting, "My ex never follows through with the kids' plans," you might say, "It's challenging when plans change unexpectedly and affect the kids. I just want to make sure they have stability." This way, you're sharing your experience without making it about blaming your ex, which can help friends understand your situation without feeling caught in the middle.

It's also crucial to set clear boundaries about what personal information you're comfortable sharing, especially if your friends still hang out with your ex. For example, if you're starting a new relationship, you might not want your ex to know immediately. So, you could tell a mutual friend, "Hey, I'm seeing someone new, but

I'm not ready to share that news broadly yet. I'd appreciate it if you could keep that private for now." This helps protect your privacy and ensures that personal details don't get back to your ex, who might use them to cause problems.

Finding and leaning on trustworthy friends is vital. These people understand your situation, respect your privacy, and offer genuine support. For example, maybe you have a friend who checks in with you after a rough co-parenting week just to see how you're doing. Or perhaps a neighbor offers to watch the kids for a few hours so you can have some time to yourself. These friends become a vital support system, offering a listening ear and practical help when things get overwhelming. They help you maintain a sense of normalcy and remind you that you're not alone. By building these supportive relationships, you create a buffer against the challenges of co-parenting, making it easier to navigate the ups and downs.

9.3 Educating Family and Friends on Narcissism

When co-parenting with a difficult ex, close friends and family support can make a huge difference. But understanding narcissism can be tricky for many, so it's helpful to explain it clearly so they can genuinely support you. You might want to share easy-to-read articles, insightful books, and informative workshops. Look for books that cover the psychological aspects of narcissism and include personal stories from people who have been through it. This can provide deeper insight and empathy. Workshops led by mental health professionals can also be great—they offer an interactive way to understand narcissistic behaviors and how to deal with them effectively.

It is essential to set realistic expectations with your friends and family about what they might experience when interacting with your ex. Let them know that some behaviors may seem unsettling or confusing but that these actions are often part of the narcissistic disorder. To help them understand better, share specific scenarios they might encounter. For example, your ex might try to sway people's opinions of you or turn a friendly conversation into a critique of you or your parenting.

Explaining these potential behaviors prepares your friends and family for what they might face. This preparation can help them stay calm and composed, even if your ex tries to provoke a reaction. It's about helping them understand that these behaviors are not about them but a part of how your ex may try to control or manipulate situations. This understanding allows them to support you and your children better without unintentionally escalating the situation. Being prepared also helps them respond in a way that keeps the focus on creating a peaceful and supportive environment for everyone involved.

Encourage your friends and family to be supportive by offering concrete examples of how they can help. For instance, they can change the subject if a conversation becomes tense or stay close to you if your ex tries to dominate or intimidate you. If they witness inappropriate behavior, such as your ex making snide remarks or trying to alienate you in front of others, guide them on how to intervene gently and tactfully. This could involve suggesting a break in the conversation, redirecting the topic, or discreetly helping you and your kids step away from a stressful situation.

Sometimes, friends or family might not fully grasp the impact of narcissistic behavior, especially if they've only seen the charming side of your ex. It can be challenging when they don't understand what's happening, but sharing specific examples can help. For instance, you could explain how your ex blames you for everything, even when it's completely unreasonable—like saying you caused the child to become severely ill with vomiting and fever just because you allowed them to eat a few Oreo cookies for a snack. This blame game can make you and the kids feel guilty and confused, adding unnecessary stress and tension at home.

By explaining these situations calmly and clearly, you help your friends and family understand what's going on without making it seem like you're trying to turn them against your ex. Respecting their relationships and feelings is important, so focus on sharing your experiences and setting boundaries rather than trying to change their opinions. They can support you and your kids without feeling pressured to pick sides.

Educating and preparing your friends and family creates a more informed and empathetic support network. This approach ensures that when they interact with your ex, they know what to expect and can handle situations in a way that supports your family's well-being. A shared understanding and strategy provide a stronger, united front that upholds the values of respect and empathy, making it easier for everyone involved to navigate the complexities of co-parenting with a narcissist.

9.4 Building a Positive Community for You and Your Children

Creating a nurturing environment for you and your children goes beyond managing co-parenting challenges. It's about surrounding your family with a supportive community. Joining groups that understand your situation can significantly enhance your support system. Look for parenting groups, especially those for single parents or those dealing with high-conflict co-parenting. These groups offer emotional support and practical advice tailored to your needs. Sharing experiences and strategies with others in similar situations can reduce feelings of isolation. Local chapters of parenting groups or online communities focused on narcissistic abuse recovery can provide valuable understanding and support.

Support groups specifically for single parents or those dealing with narcissistic abuse offer a safe space to express challenges and learn from others. These groups often have discussions led by professionals who provide guidance and coping strategies. Joining these groups can help you feel less alone and more understood. They support your emotional healing and give you practical tools to handle co-parenting challenges.

Volunteering and engaging in community activities help build a supportive network while teaching your children the value of community involvement. Participate in local events, charity functions, or school activities to expand your social circle. These activities can lead to friendships with people with similar values or experiences. Being active in the community can strengthen your sense of belonging and purpose. For children, seeing their parents involved in positive community roles teaches them the importance of giving back and being part of a community.

Creating or participating in inclusive events also fosters a supportive environment. Organize or join community events that celebrate diversity and inclusivity. These events should welcome all families, especially those facing extra challenges. Events can include cultural festivals, parent-child workshops at the local library, or community picnics. Being part of these initiatives enriches your social life and reinforces the values of acceptance and support. These experiences counteract feelings of isolation and help create a positive outlook for your family.

Using community resources can ease the stresses of single parenting and recovering from complicated relationships. Many communities offer resources like counseling services, educational programs, and recreational activities to support families in challenging situations. Contact local community centers, schools, or mental health organizations to find resources to help your family's needs. These include parenting classes, mental health counseling, or arts and sports programs for children. These resources provide practical support and opportunities for emotional growth and healing.

Building a positive community involves engaging with supportive networks, participating in community activities, and using available resources. This enhances your and your children's quality of life and shows the importance of community support and resilience. By actively engaging with your community, you create a nurturing environment that helps buffer the stressors of co-parenting and paves the way for a healthier, more fulfilled family life.

Remember, a community's strength lies in its ability to uplift and support its members through all seasons of life. By embedding yourself and your children in a positive, active community, you lay down roots in a nurturing environment. This community can provide shelter from life's storms and allow you all to flourish despite challenges. In the next chapter, we will focus on embracing future possibilities and ensuring the path forward is enriching and empowering.

TEN

Self-Care

S tepping into the world of self-care, especially after a high-conflict divorce, can feel like entering a calm space after a storm. It's about nurturing yourself to heal from the past and empower yourself for the future. This chapter is about making self-care a fundamental part of your emotional, mental, and physical well-being journey.

10.1 Self-Care: Essential, Not Optional

When coping with a challenging ex-partner, self-care means more than spa days and treats. It's about building a solid foundation that supports your overall well-being. Recognize that your health is the cornerstone of your family's happiness and resilience. Self-care involves a comprehensive approach: physical health, mental clarity, and emotional strength. It's about finding peace, strength, and joy in your everyday life.

Prioritizing self-care is essential. The emotional and psychological demands of co-parenting with a narcissist can leave you feeling burned out, isolated, and completely drained. Making self-care a priority is like putting on your oxygen mask first; it's necessary, not selfish. By ensuring your well-being, you handle stress better, make clear decisions, and provide the emotional support your children need.

Integrate simple yet effective self-care practices into your daily routine. Mindfulness exercises can bring calm to a chaotic day. Focus on the present moment, acknowledging your thoughts and feelings without judgment. Just a few minutes of mindfulness daily can reduce stress and increase emotional resilience.

Journaling offers a private space to express thoughts and emotions. Write about your day, feelings, and interactions with your ex to process emotions and gain perspective. This practice can help you identify patterns and handle future interactions more effectively.

Regular physical activity releases endorphins, improving mood and reducing depression and anxiety. Find an activity you enjoy, whether a walk in the park, a yoga session, or a dance class, and make it a part of your daily routine.

Treat self-care activities with the same importance as other responsibilities. Set aside specific times for mindfulness, journaling, and exercise. This structured approach ensures that self-care becomes a consistent part of your routine, providing stability and strength as you navigate co-parenting challenges.

By embracing self-care, you cope better with your situation and model healthy habits for your children. They learn from watching you that caring for one's health is essential, even in difficult times. This chapter is not just about sustaining you—it's about inspiring those you love to prioritize their well-being.

10.2 Stress Relief Techniques

Dealing with a difficult ex can bring many challenges, from emotional outbursts to legal battles. These situations can be very stressful, but identifying what triggers your stress can help you manage your mental health. For example, you might feel anxious when receiving contentious emails from your ex or dread preparing for custody exchanges. Inconsistent parenting decisions can also be frustrating, especially when they negatively affect the children. Recognizing these triggers is the first step in developing strategies to cope with them and minimize their impact on your life.

To manage stress, you can use various techniques. For instance, deep breathing exercises can help you calm down quickly during tense moments. When you feel overwhelmed, try taking slow, deliberate breaths, counting to four as you inhale, holding for four counts, and then exhaling for four counts. This simple exercise can activate your body's natural relaxation response, helping you regain composure. Meditation offers a deeper level of relaxation and mental clarity. By setting aside even 10 minutes a day for meditation, you can cultivate mindfulness, allowing you to observe your thoughts and feelings without judgment. This practice can be beneficial when dealing with the emotional ups and downs of co-parenting with a difficult ex.

Maintaining a balanced diet and getting enough sleep is essential for managing stress. Nutritious foods can boost your immune system, reduce blood pressure, and stabilize moods. For example, incorporating fatty fish like salmon, rich in omega-3 fatty acids, can help reduce inflammation and improve brain function. Leafy greens, nuts, and seeds provide essential nutrients for overall health. Sleep is equally important; aim for 7-9 hours of quality sleep each night. Lack of sleep can exacerbate stress and make it harder to manage your emotions. Establish a bedtime routine with winding down activities like reading a book or taking a warm bath to signal your body that it's time to rest.

Making time for hobbies and relaxation is crucial. This time should be non-negotiable and prioritized just like any other responsibility. Whether you enjoy reading, painting, hiking, or gardening, make time for activities that bring you joy and allow you to unwind. For example, if you love gardening, planting flowers or tending to your vegetable garden can be a therapeutic way to disconnect from daily stressors. Communicate the importance of this personal time to those around you and set clear boundaries to protect it. Let your family and friends know this is your time to recharge and ask for their support in respecting this boundary.

If stress becomes overwhelming, seeking professional help can be a valuable resource. Therapists or counselors experienced in high-conflict relationships can provide tools and strategies to manage stress. They can help you develop new coping mechanisms, offer support during difficult times, and provide a safe space to express your feelings. For example, a therapist might teach you cognitive-behavioral techniques to challenge negative thoughts and replace them with more positive ones. They can also help you navigate the complexities of co-parenting and offer advice on communicating more effectively with your ex.

By integrating these mental health practices into your daily routine, you can better cope with stressors and enhance your overall well-being. Taking care of your mental health makes you more resilient and better equipped to handle the challenges of co-parenting with a difficult ex. This approach benefits you and helps you be a more present and supportive parent for your children, creating a more stable and nurturing environment for them to thrive in.

10.3 Finding Time for Yourself

Finding time for yourself while co-parenting can feel almost impossible, but it's crucial. It's all about creating moments of peace and renewal in your busy life. Good time management, focusing on meaningful activities, and making the most of child-free times are critical.

Start by reviewing your daily schedule and finding gaps where you can incorporate self-care. Plan your week and use a calendar on your phone or a physical one to set aside time just for you. Make these moments a priority, choosing activities that help you recharge and feel good.

When it comes to self-care, quality is more important than quantity. Even short breaks can make a big difference if you spend them doing something you love. For instance, a quick 20-minute walk in a park can be way more refreshing than spending hours scrolling through social media.

Take advantage of times when your kids are at school, asleep, or with your ex. Use these moments to do things that lift your spirits. 'Me time' doesn't just mean being alone; it can also mean catching up with friends, taking a class, or getting involved in community events. It's about doing things that make you feel happy and fulfilled.

You're setting up a positive routine that supports your well-being by making time for yourself and focusing on quality self-care. This helps you handle the ups and downs of co-parenting better and makes your life more satisfying overall.

10.4 Emotional Healing from Abuse

This section focuses on recognizing emotional abuse and taking the first steps toward recovery. Embracing these healing practices means taking control of your life and not letting past hurts dictate your future. Healing is a journey that requires patience, understanding, and self-compassion. Each step you take, no matter how small, helps you reclaim your story and rediscover your strength. Use the tips and strategies in this chapter as a guide to navigate the challenges and find new opportunities for a healthy, fulfilling life. Remember, you deserve to be happy and free from the shadows of the past.

Recognizing emotional abuse is the first step toward healing, and it's important to acknowledge that it can take many forms. Emotional abuse often involves constant criticism, making you feel like you're never good enough. It can also involve gaslighting, where you're manipulated into doubting your memories and feelings, leaving you confused and questioning your reality. Emotional neglect happens when someone ignores your needs and emotions, making you feel invisible and unimportant. These experiences can leave deep scars, affecting your self-esteem and sense of worth. Understanding these signs helps you realize that your feelings are valid and that the pain you're experiencing has a source - one that isn't your fault.

The good news is that there are many ways to heal and recover from emotional abuse. One practical approach is psychotherapy, especially trauma-focused therapy. This type of therapy helps you process your experiences, understand how they've impacted you, and develop strategies to move forward. For example, a therapist might help you work through painful memories and teach you coping mechanisms for managing anxiety or depression. Art therapy can also be a great option, providing a creative outlet to express emotions that might be hard to put into words. Art therapy can be a safe space to explore and release your feelings, whether through painting, drawing, or even music.

Participating in a supportive community or spiritual practices, like meditation or prayer, can offer a sense of connection and purpose. Being part of a community, whether a spiritual group or a supportive circle of friends, can help you feel less alone and more understood. Meditation can help you find inner peace and clarity, while a prayer might provide comfort and a sense of hope. It's about finding practices that resonate with you and help you feel grounded.

Journaling is another powerful tool for self-reflection. Writing down your thoughts and feelings can help you make sense of your experiences and track your healing journey. It's a private space where you can be completely honest with yourself. As you reflect on your entries, you may start seeing patterns and progress you hadn't noticed before. And remember, celebrating small victories is important. Maybe you stood up for yourself in a situation where you would have stayed silent before, or perhaps you simply had a day where you felt more at peace. No matter how small, these moments are signs of your growing strength and resilience.

ELEVEN

Building a New Future

I magine standing at the beginning of a new journey full of
opportunities and hope. This chapter is about stepping into that
space where your past, with all its challenges, becomes a backdrop
to a fresh start. Moving forward, the heavy weight of your previous
experiences begins to lift, revealing a path filled with opportunities
for rediscovery and renewal. Here, we explore how to redefine your
identity, focusing on the resilience and growth you've gained.

11.1 Redefining Your Identity

Untangling yourself from a tricky relationship can feel like hitting
the reset button. It's all about peeling away the doubts and
rediscovering who you are. This process shows your strength and
helps you regain control of your life.

During the relationship, you felt like you were in the background,
and your needs didn't matter. Now that you're stepping out of that
shadow take a moment to acknowledge the personal growth you've
achieved. Think about the strengths you've developed, like sharper
intuition, greater empathy, or the courage to set boundaries. These

are valuable lessons you've gained from your challenging experiences.

To reconnect with who you are, dive back into your interests and values. Get involved in activities you loved before or always wanted to try. Whether painting, hiking, writing, or volunteering, these activities help you rediscover parts of yourself you may have pushed aside.

Exploring your passions and interests isn't just about having fun— it's a way to rebuild your self-esteem and independence. It brings back joy and excitement, which are critical to a happy life. So, why not join a dance class, a book club, or start a gardening project? Pick something that makes you feel alive and dive in.

With a better understanding of yourself, start setting new personal goals. These could be career aspirations or personal development targets like getting healthier or learning a new language. Ensure these goals inspire and give you a sense of purpose and direction.

Surround yourself with people who support and affirm the new you. This could be old friends, new ones who share your interests, or family members who offer unconditional love. Keep these relationships strong with open communication about your needs and boundaries.

Finally, take time to celebrate your independence. This isn't just about leaving a relationship but starting a new chapter. Celebrate the small wins, the daily reminders of your strength, and the freedom to make choices that honor your well-being.

As you go through these steps, remember that each is integral to rebuilding a life that genuinely reflects who you are. This isn't just about moving on from a burdensome relationship; it's about stepping into a future that aligns with your deepest desires and values. By embracing these changes, you're not just surviving— you're thriving and creating a life where you can truly belong and find happiness.

11.2 Planning for a Narcissist-Free Future

As you move forward, you must clearly understand what you want your future to look like. This isn't just about dreaming—it's about making it happen. Start thinking about what would make you happy, both personally and professionally. Picture yourself making essential decisions, celebrating successes, and prioritizing your well-being. One way to start is by creating a vision board or writing a detailed life plan. Think about where you'd like to live, the kind of work you'd enjoy, and how you'd like to spend your time. This vision will keep you focused and motivated, especially when feeling down about the past.

Being financially independent is another vital part of your new life. It's not just about covering bills; it's about building a safety net for you and your kids. Financial planning can include investing in stocks, mutual funds, or retirement accounts to ensure your financial growth aligns with your personal goals.

Creating a supportive environment is also really important. Surround yourself with people who understand where you've been and support where you're going. Make your home a place that reflects your new beginnings and encourages your growth. This could mean setting up a home office that motivates you, a quiet spot for meditation, or a cozy living area that brings you joy. Beyond your home, look for a community that shares your interests and values. Whether it's local groups, online forums, or social clubs, these connections offer companionship and networking opportunities for personal and professional growth.

Embracing your future means learning from your past and building a life that truly feels like yours. With a clear vision and solid emotional and financial strategies, you'll be on your way to a life where you feel empowered, stable, and free to pursue happiness on your terms.

11.3 Building Resilience In Your Children

Raising kids after leaving a complicated relationship means helping them become strong and adaptable. As a parent, you provide care and love and teach them to handle life's challenges. Building resilience in your kids involves giving them the tools they need to thrive, even when things get tough.

You can start by making problem-solving fun, like a game or puzzle. For instance, if a toy breaks or they disagree with a friend, guide them through figuring out the problem, coming up with solutions, and picking the best one. This helps them solve the problem and gives them a sense of accomplishment and independence.

Another critical aspect is teaching emotional regulation. Help your kids understand and manage their emotions by showing them simple techniques like deep breathing or counting to ten when upset. Encourage them to express their feelings through talking, drawing, or playing, which can help them process and understand their emotions.

It's also important to talk about what they learn from different experiences. After something happens, discuss what went well, what could be better, and what they learned. This helps them develop a mindset that values growth and learning from challenges.

As their parent, you're their most important role model. Show them how you handle challenging situations with grace and determination. Share age-appropriate stories about your challenges and how you overcame them. When they see you bounce back from setbacks, they'll learn resilience is about getting back up and trying again.

Encouraging independence is also vital. Give your kids the chance to make decisions and solve problems. Start with small choices, like picking out their clothes or choosing a game to play. As they age, involve them in more significant decisions and responsibilities, like taking care of a pet or managing their allowance. This teaches them accountability and the satisfaction of personal achievement.

Family traditions can be a great way to celebrate resilience and strength. For example, have regular family meetings where everyone shares the highs and lows of the week, focusing on personal strengths or lessons learned. Engage in activities like hiking or team sports that build perseverance and teamwork. Celebrate milestones and achievements by recognizing the results and the effort it took. These traditions help reinforce the values you want to instill in your kids.

Teaching empathy is also crucial. Use everyday situations to help your kids understand different feelings and perspectives. Encourage them to think about how others feel and respond with kindness. You can role-play various scenarios, discussing handling tricky situations with empathy and assertiveness. This helps them develop resilience and compassion, especially in understanding and dealing with challenging behavior from others.

Finally, create a safe space for your kids to express their emotions. Encourage open communication by sharing your feelings and inviting them to share theirs. Listen without judgment and show them that their feelings matter. Offer tools like journals, art supplies, or music to help them express and process their emotions. This openness helps them feel confident in sharing and managing their feelings.

By guiding your kids through these practices, you're helping them grow into well-rounded, emotionally intelligent individuals. This legacy of resilience, independence, and empathy is one of the greatest gifts you can give, preparing them to face the world confidently.

11.4 Creating a Peaceful Future

Building a peaceful and calm future starts with having a clear idea of what that looks like for you. Picture a day where everything feels right—morning light fills your home, and there's a lot of laughter and understanding. Imagine your interactions with your kids being joyful and your personal space radiating the tranquility you've always wanted. This isn't just a daydream; it's the beginning of the life you're creating.

To make this vision a reality, consider what makes up your ideal day, like a smooth morning routine or peaceful time with your kids. Break these down into steps you can do. For instance, if mornings feel hectic, figure out what's causing the chaos and work on fixing it. This could be as simple as better time management or tidying up your living space.

Another critical step is creating a positive living environment. Look around your current space—does it feel calm or chaotic? Make changes that promote relaxation and happiness. This could mean decluttering, adding plants, or setting up a cozy reading nook. Think about using soothing colors like soft blues or greens in your decor. A tidy and peaceful home can make it easier to maintain a calm mindset.

As you start incorporating these elements into your life, each day brings you closer to the future you envision. It's about creating a life that prioritizes peace and fulfillment. This journey isn't just about leaving behind a complicated past; it's about moving toward a future where you're the priority. Remember these tips and strategies as you build a life filled with peace, stability, and happiness.

Afterword

As we end our journey together, let's take a moment to reflect on what we've learned. We've covered everything from understanding narcissism and its impact on relationships, navigating legal challenges, establishing effective communication strategies, and practicing self-care. This journey has been about moving from feeling overwhelmed to feeling empowered and clear-headed.

We discussed the importance of empathy and keeping hope alive in the beginning. Co-parenting with a difficult ex isn't easy, but remember, there is always a way forward. I wrote this book to give you strategies, offer comfort, and remind you that you're not alone.

Throughout the book, we've explored various strategies for effective co-parenting, even in challenging situations. These strategies are robust, but they need flexibility. Life changes, and so will the methods you use. Stay adaptable and ready to adjust as your co-parenting situation evolves.

One important takeaway is building resilience in your children. By teaching them how to handle challenges, you're giving them tools to thrive. Instilling values like empathy and the importance of healthy relationships will benefit them throughout their lives.

Your support network is vital. Friends, family, and support groups offer emotional and practical help that makes a big difference. Through these networks, you can share and learn about the changing nature of co-parenting and dealing with problematic behavior.

This book has given you knowledge, and with knowledge comes power. Each strategy you use is a step toward a more confident and resilient you. Keep learning, growing, and letting your new understanding guide you in co-parenting.

Looking ahead, hold on to hope. The challenges are real, but a peaceful and rewarding co-parenting environment is possible. Your dedication to creating a stable, loving home for yourself and your children is inspiring.

I encourage you to connect with others who share your experiences. There's great strength in community and shared understanding. Join online forums support groups, and use social media to reach out to others in similar situations.

Thank you for joining me on this journey. Your determination to seek knowledge and strategies for better co-parenting shows your strength. I hope you'll share your stories and feedback as you apply what you have learned. Your insights are invaluable to others in similar situations.

Remember your strength and resilience. The road may be tough, but you are tougher. You have the tools and the heart to create a nurturing, peaceful life for yourself and your children. Keep moving forward with hope and courage, knowing you can navigate the challenges of co-parenting with grace and wisdom.

As you've explored the challenges and strategies for co-parenting with a narcissist, you've gained insights and tools to make this journey a bit smoother. Now, it's your turn to share your experience and help others facing similar situations.

By leaving a genuine review of this book on Amazon, you can be a guiding light for others navigating the complex world of co-parenting with a narcissistic partner. Your feedback will help them find practical advice and support, empowering them to create a healthier environment for themselves and their children.

Thank you for your support. Co-parenting is never easy, but together, we can make it more manageable for everyone involved.

Bibliography

- *Narcissistic Personality Disorder* https://emedicine.medscape.com/article/1519417-overview
- *How Narcissistic Parenting Can Affect Children* https://www.psychologytoday.com/us/blog/the-legacy-of-distorted-love/201802/how-narcissistic-parenting-can-affect-children
- *How to Communicate With a Narcissist* https://www.psychologytoday.com/us/blog/stress-fracture/202212/how-to-communicate-with-a-narcissist
- *The challenges of co-parenting with a narcissist - Family Law* https://www.beermannfamilylaw.com/blog/2022/06/the-challenges-of-co-parenting-with-a-narcissist/
- *Best evidence for child custody cases* https://www.custodyxchange.com/topics/custody/steps/best-evidence-custody.php
- *Co-Parenting With a Narcissist: Tips and Strategies* https://www.custodyxchange.com/topics/custody/special-circumstances/co-parenting-with-narcissist.php
- *Hiring a Lawyer Who Understands High Conflict* https://highconflictinstitute.com/divorce-coparenting/chapter-7-hiring-a-lawyer-who-understands/
- *How to Negotiate Child Support with a Narcissist?* https://www.judgeanthony.com/blog/how-to-negotiate-child-support-with-a-narcissist
- *4-Part Nonviolent Communication (NVC)* https://www.nonviolentcommunication.com/learn-nonviolent-communication/4-part-nvc/
- *The Grey Rock Method: A Technique for Handling Toxic ...* https://psychcentral.com/health/grey-rock-method
- *Co-Parenting Communication Guide* https://parentinganddivorceclass.com/wp-content/uploads/2017/03/AFCC-Coparenting-Communication-Guide.pdf
- *How Technology Can Help You Be a Better Co-Parent ...* https://elisebuiefamilylaw.com/how-technology-can-help-you-be-a-better-co-parent-parent-team/
- *How to Set Boundaries With a Narcissist* https://www.charliehealth.com/post/how-to-set-boundaries-with-a-narcissist
- *Setting Boundaries with a High Conflict Co-Parent* https://www.ourfamilywizard.com/blog/setting-boundaries-high-conflict-co-parent
- *Children of Narcissistic Parents: Effects, Healing, and More* https://www.healthline.com/health/mental-health/children-of-narcissistic-parents
- *Co-Parenting With a Toxic Ex: 10 Tips From a Therapist* https://www.choosingtherapy.com/co-parenting-with-a-toxic-ex/
- *Children of Narcissistic Parents: Effects, Healing, and More* https://www.healthline.com/health/mental-health/children-of-narcissistic-parents
- *19+ Innovative Ways to Teach Emotional Intelligence to Kids* https://positivepsychology.com/emotional-intelligence-for-kids/

Bibliography

- *Helping Children Cope With a Narcissistic Parent* https://www.psychologytoday.com/us/blog/living-on-automatic/202301/helping-children-cope-with-a-narcissistic-parent
- *The Effects of Divorce on Children & How to Help them Cope* https://www.psych.uic.edu/research/community-based-children-and-family-mental-health-services-research-program/in-the-news/the-effects-of-divorce-on-children-how-to-help-them-cope
- *Stress relievers: Tips to tame stress* https://www.mayoclinic.org/healthy-lifestyle/stress-management/in-depth/stress-relievers/art-20047257
- *Healing from Narcissistic Abuse: The Role of Cognitive ...* https://mark-havens.medium.com/healing-from-narcissistic-abuse-the-role-of-cognitive-behavioral-therapy-5f34630710a1
- *Ask a Therapist: "How to Set Boundaries With a Narcissist"* https://www.talkspace.com/mental-health/conditions/articles/how-to-set-boundaries-with-a-narcissist/
- *How to Find a Narcissistic Abuse Support Group* https://www.verywellmind.com/how-to-find-a-narcissistic-abuse-support-group-5271477
- *Financial Abuse: How to Recognize It and Tips to Cope ...* https://psychcentral.com/health/financial-abuse
- *Financial Independence After Divorce: A Step-by-Step Guide* https://splytup.com/financial-independence-after-divorce-a-step-by-step-guide/
- *How Are Divorce Settlements Calculated?* https://www.findlaw.com/family/divorce/how-are-divorce-settlements-calculated.html
- *Navigating Life Events: Divorced Spouse Resources* https://www.benefits.gov/news/article/468
- *Parallel Parenting: An Alternative Approach for High-Conflict ...* https://freedmarcroft.com/parallel-parenting-an-alternative-approach-for-high-conflict-co-parents/#:~:text=Benefits%20of%20Parallel%20Parenting&text=By%20establishing%20separate%20routines%20and,negative%20effects%20of%20ongoing%20conflict.
- *Parallel Parenting: Making a Plan and Getting Started* https://www.custodyxchange.com/topics/custody/advice/parallel-parenting.php#:~:text=If%20you're%20able%20to,order%20both%20parents%20must%20follow.
- *Parallel Parenting: Strategies for High-Conflict Co-Parenting* https://prolegalcare.com/parallel-parenting-strategies-for-high-conflict-co-parenting/
- *Separated parents' ways to coparent and promote ...* https://www.ncbi.nlm.nih.gov/pmc/articles/PMC6457541/
- *The narcissist under the hood - The difficulty of explaining ...* https://loveandabuse.com/the-narcissist-under-the-hood-the-difficulty-of-explaining-emotional-abuse-to-friends-and-family/
- *Cybersecurity for Co-Parents: How You Can Protect Yourself ...* https://www.ourfamilywizard.com/blog/cybersecurity-co-parents-how-you-can-protect-yourself-digital-world
- *More connections, less stress can help single parents do their ...* https://www.

firstthingsfirst.org/first-things/more-connections-less-stress-can-help-single-parents-do-their-best/

- *Empowering You in Mediation with a Narcissistic Ex-Partner* https://aspirefamilymediation.co.uk/empowering-you-in-mediation-with-a-narcissistic-ex-partner/
- *7 Ways to Set Boundaries With Narcissists* https://www.psychologytoday.com/us/blog/narcissism-demystified/202006/7-ways-set-boundaries-narcissists
- *8 Guidelines to Guard Yourself from a Narcissist in Divorce* - https://www.micklinlawgroup.com/8-guidelines-guard-yourself-from-narcissist-divorce/
- *Creating a Perfect Parenting Plan in 6 Steps* https://www.ourfamilywizard.com/blog/creating-perfect-parenting-plan-6-steps
- *Supporting Kids During a Divorce - Child Mind Institute* https://childmind.org/article/supporting-kids-during-a-divorce/#:~:text=The%20best%20thing%20parents%20-can%20do%20to%20help%20kids%20cope,why%20you%20feel%20that%20way.